Mastering Inventory

W9-BYV-327

by
Philip E. Meyer, CPA, DBA
Professor of Accounting
Boston University

Philip E. Meyer, CPA, DBA, is Professor of Accounting, Boston University, Boston, Massachusetts. He has published in academic and professional journals, including *The CPA Journal, Practical Accountant, Massachusetts CPA Review, The Accounting Review, Accounting Horizons,* and *Journal of Accounting Research.*

Publisher and Editor
Stephen Sahlein

Consulting Editor
L.G. Schloss
Iona College (Retired)

AIPB Advisory Board

Dr. Gary F. Bulmash
Department of Accounting
American University

Barry C. Broden, DBA, CPA
University of Hartford

Dr. Gordon S. May
J.M. Tull School
of Accounting (Emeritus)
University of Georgia

Simon, Krowitz & Bolin, CPAs
Rockville, MD

Design: Moss Design, Bethesda, MD
Typesetting: Lovelady Consulting, Roswell, GA

INTRODUCTION

Mastering Inventory covers everything you need to know for the inventory portion of the *Certified Bookkeeper* examination. If you take the optional open-book Final Examination at the end of this workbook, return the answer sheet to AIPB and achieve a grade of at least 70, then become a *Certified Bookkeeper* within three years, you will receive retroactively ten (10) Continuing Professional Education Credits (CPECs) toward the *Certified Bookkeeper* continuing education requirements. You will also receive promptly an AIPB *Certificate of Completion*.

If you are not an applicant for the *Certified Bookkeeper* designation and take the optional open-book Final Examination at the end of this workbook, return the answer sheet to AIPB and achieve a grade of at least 70, you will receive an AIPB *Certificate of Completion*.

When you have completed this course, you should be able to:

1. Record inventory purchases and sales and determine cost of goods sold and ending inventory under the perpetual method.

2. Record inventory purchases and sales and determine cost of goods sold and ending inventory under the periodic method.

3. Compute and record cost of goods sold and ending inventory using weighted average and moving average costing.

4. Compute and record cost of goods sold and ending inventory using first-in, first-out (FIFO) costing.

5. Compute and record cost of goods sold and ending inventory using last-in, first-out (LIFO) costing.

6. Compute and record changes in inventory under the lower of cost or market (LCM) rule.

To get the most out of the course, we suggest the following:

1. Read the concise narrative that begins each section.

2. Read the narrative again. This time, cover the solution and try to figure out each problem. Actually write it out. By *trying* to solve the problem and checking your answer against the correct solution, you will learn a great deal.

3. Take Quiz #1 at the end of each section to see what you learned and what you need to review.

4. Take Quiz #2 at the end of each section to master any points you missed.

Lastly, please take a moment to fill out and send in the Course Evaluation at the back (whether or not you take the final). It will help us to improve this and other courses.

Enjoy the course—and congratulations on taking a major step toward advancing your professional knowledge and career.

CONTENTS

Certified Bookkeeper Applicants

The best way to study for the certification exam is to take each section's quizzes over and over until you can answer questions quickly and comfortably—*and* know why the answer is correct. If you have trouble with a question, or know the answer, but not why it is correct, review the related material. Write answers on a separate sheet, wherever possible, to avoid seeing them each time you take the quiz.

INTRODUCTION TO ACCOUNTING FOR INVENTORY

Manufacturing Companies v. Merchandising Companies

The inventory asset is merchandise owned by a company. How inventory is classified depends on whether the company is a *manufacturing company* or a *merchandising company* (a retailer or a distributor).

A *manufacturing company* buys raw materials for processing into a finished product. Manufacturing inventories include raw materials inventory, work-in-process inventory, and finished goods inventory (completed items held for sale). The area of accounting that covers manufacturing inventory costs is called *cost accounting* and is not included in this course.

A *merchandising company* holds inventory for resale. When it holds different kinds of inventory, the items held for resale are technically referred to as *merchandise inventory,* but in practice are called simply *inventories* or *inventory.* This course covers merchandise inventory.

Recording Merchandise Purchase Costs

<u>What</u> *is included in purchase costs*

The cost of inventory is the purchase amount actually paid to the seller—not the price in a catalog or on the purchase order. If cash is not paid immediately, the purchase is recorded *on account*. Costs such as transportation and insurance that are part of merchandise costs are recorded as inventory costs and are known as *inventoriable costs.*

<u>When</u> *purchase costs are recorded*

Merchandise is recorded on the books when the buyer obtains "legal title" to the goods. Legal title generally passes from seller to buyer when the goods leave the seller's premises (*shipping point*) or when they arrive at the

---

buyer's premises (*destination*). This is usually specified in the purchase contract as follows:

- **F.O.B. (free on board) shipping point** means that the buyer obtains legal title when the goods leave the seller's premises. The freight and insurance costs are incurred by the buyer.

- **F.O.B. destination** means that the buyer obtains legal title when the goods arrive at the buyer's premises. The freight and insurance costs are incurred by the seller.

Placing an order for a delivery is not an accounting event (unless the buyer makes a deposit), so it is not recorded on the books. In practice, many companies record a purchase when they receive the invoice. This is generally harmless unless it occurs at year end. Purchases made near year end *must* be recorded in the year in which legal title is acquired.

For example, on December 10, 20X4, your company places two orders F.O.B. destination (legal title passes to your company when the goods arrive). Order #1 arrives on December 28, 20X4, and Order #2 arrives on January 2, 20X5. You receive the invoices for both orders on January 10, 20X5. You *must* record Order #1 on the 20X4 books as a purchase because you obtained legal title to the goods on December 28, 20X4. You *must* record Order #2 on your 20X5 books as a purchase because you obtained legal title to the goods on January 2, 20X5.

Other inventoriable costs

The buyer that pays freight and insurance includes both as inventoriable costs (purchase costs). This is true whether the buyer pays the seller for shipping or directly pays the carrier. If the seller incurs the freight and insurance, the buyer does not include these as inventoriable costs.

When the carrier requires payment in advance or on delivery, the cash outlay for freight and insurance may be made by the buyer even though the seller agreed to incur this cost.

Use the following facts for Problems 1–3: Your company buys merchandise from a wholesaler for $4,000; the freight cost is $200.

PROBLEM 1: Your sales contract specifies F.O.B. destination. What cost does your company record for the merchandise?

SOLUTION 1: Your company records $4,000 as the cost of the merchandise because the seller incurred the freight cost.

PROBLEM 2: Your sales contract specifies F.O.B. shipping point, and your company pays the carrier. What cost does your company record for the merchandise?

SOLUTION 2: Your company records $4,200 as the cost of the merchandise because your company (the buyer) incurred the freight cost.

PROBLEM 3: Your sales contract specifies F.O.B. shipping point and your wholesaler paid the carrier in advance for the delivery. What cost does your company record for the merchandise?

SOLUTION 3: Your company records $4,200 as the cost of the merchandise because your company (the buyer) incurred the freight cost. Your company will reimburse the wholesaler.

Financial Statements Reporting

Reporting on the income statement. The cost of merchandise sold during the year is recognized as an expense—either *cost of goods sold* or *cost of sales*—but the word "inventory" does not appear on the income statement.

If, however, the cost of goods sold computation appears on the income statement, "inventory" will appear as follows:

```
Beginning inventory
+   Purchases
Cost of goods available for sale
–   Ending inventory
Cost of goods sold
```

Reporting on the balance sheet. Merchandise on hand at the end of the year appears on the balance sheet as an asset (inventory asset) under *current assets*. The dollar value of this asset includes all inventoriable costs for goods on hand at year end (such as freight and insurance). The calculations used to determine this value are explained in this course.

PROBLEM 4: In your company's first year of business, it buys merchandise for $50,000. It sells a portion of the goods that cost $30,000 for $75,000. Which amounts should appear on the balance sheet and income statement at year end?

SOLUTION 4:

Balance sheet:
Inventory $20,000[1]

Income statement:
Sales revenue $75,000
Cost of goods sold   −30,000
Gross profit[2] $45,000

[1] $50,000 merchandise purchased − $30,000 merchandise sold = $20,000 merchandise in ending inventory.

[2] The term "gross margin" is also used.

What Did the Inventory That Was Sold Cost the Company?

The totals that go on the income statement as sales revenue and cost of goods sold, and on the balance sheet as inventory, are simple to show. But inventory costs can be difficult—or even impossible—to figure out.

For example, a hardware store buys hundreds of screwdrivers throughout the year. It purchases 75 screwdrivers on January 7 at $0.57 each, 42 on January 20 at $0.47 each, and 37 on February 4 at $0.42 each. It continues to make similar purchases throughout the year. On November 5, it sells a screwdriver for $1.10. How can the store know that particular screwdriver's cost?

The answer is that it cannot. This is what accounting for inventory is all about: coming up with the cost of merchandise sold during the year (to record on the income statement as cost of goods sold) and the cost of merchandise still on hand at year end (to record on the balance sheet as ending inventory).

Most companies compute inventory costs for their financial statements by using one of several *costing methods*. These methods use *historical cost* (the actual or original cost of the items reflected in purchases made throughout the year) as a starting point. This course describes how to use various costing methods to compute the cost of inventory sold (cost of goods sold) and the cost of inventory on hand at year end (ending inventory).

- ***The costing method does not have to reflect how merchandise actually flows in and out of the company.*** For example, a company sells old merchandise before new merchandise. For accounting purposes, the company's costing method may assume that each sale includes a mix of old and new units.

- ***Once a company selects a costing method, it is expected to use that method in subsequent years.*** Although in certain circumstances, a company may change from one method to another, generally accepted accounting principles (GAAP) require that once a method is chosen, it is to be used consistently.

Of the different costing methods, only the *specific identification method* uses the actual cost of each item sold. Auto dealers can use it because they know what they paid for each car they sell since the auto's serial number is on the manufacturer's invoice to the dealer. Because most items cannot be tracked this way, the vast majority of companies are unable to use this method.

QUIZ 1   INTRODUCTION TO ACCOUNTING FOR INVENTORY

Problem I.

Fill in the blanks.

1. Costs included in merchandise costs are called _____ costs.

2. The expense of merchandise sold is referred to as the _____ _____ _____ _____ or _____ _____ _____.

3. Inventory is presented on the balance sheet under _____ _____.

Problem II.

Multiple Choice. Circle the correct answer.

1. The costing method that a company selects . . .

    a. must reflect how merchandise actually moves in and out of the company
    b. need not reflect how merchandise actually moves in and out of the company
    c. is related to how merchandise actually moves in and out of the company
    d. can be changed as often as a company chooses

2. A company records the cost of an inventory purchase . . .

    a. when it receives the invoice
    b. when legal title has passed to it
    c. when the merchandise has been delivered to it
    d. on the delivery date specified in the purchase agreement

3. The cost of inventory is . . .

    a. the amount listed in the catalog
    b. the amount shown on the purchase order
    c. the amount shown on the purchase order plus shipping and insurance
    d. the total amount actually paid or payable

Problem III.

During its first year in business, a company bought merchandise for $44,000 cash, F.O.B. destination, and sold some of it for $90,000 on account. The cost of inventory at year end came to $13,000. Calculate (1) cost of goods sold and (2) gross profit.

QUIZ 1   Solutions and Explanations

Problem I.

1. inventoriable

2. cost of goods sold, cost of sales

3. current assets

Problem II.

1. b

2. b

3. d

Problem III.

1. $44,000   cost of goods purchased
 −13,000   cost of goods on hand
$31,000   cost of goods sold

2. $90,000   sales revenue
−31,000   cost of goods sold
$59,000   gross profit

QUIZ 2   INTRODUCTION TO ACCOUNTING FOR INVENTORY

Problem I.

Fill in the blanks.

1. F.O.B. shipping point means that freight costs are paid by the _____, and F.O.B. destination means that freight costs are paid by the _____.

2. In a company's first year of operation, the cost of _____ less the cost of ending inventory equals the cost of _____ _____.

3. Although GAAP permits changing _____ methods, it generally requires that the method chosen be used consistently.

Problem II.

Multiple Choice. Circle the correct answer.

1. When an order is placed for delivery of merchandise, it is recorded on the buyer's books.

   a. True   b. False

2. Costing methods are designed to . . .

   a. determine which costs to include in inventory
   b. compute inventory profits
   c. compute the cost of merchandise sold during the year and the cost of merchandise on hand at year end
   d. all of the above

3. When computing the cost of inventory on hand at year end for the balance sheet . . .

   a. include only the purchase price of that inventory
   b. include the purchase price of that inventory plus freight
   c. include the purchase price of that inventory plus freight and insurance
   d. include the purchase price of that inventory plus any other inventoriable costs related to the merchandise, including freight and insurance

QUIZ 2 Solutions and Explanations

Problem I.

    1. buyer, seller

    2. purchases, goods sold

    3. costing

Problem II.

    1. False
    Placing an order for a delivery is *not* an accounting event (unless the buyer makes a deposit) and therefore is not recorded on the books.

    2. c

    3. d

Section 2

INVENTORY RECORDKEEPING USING THE PERPETUAL METHOD

Introduction

There are two methods of maintaining a company's inventory records: the *perpetual method* and the *periodic method*. This section covers the perpetual method.

In using the *perpetual method* to maintain inventory records, merchandise purchases and cost of goods sold are entered directly into the company's Inventory account throughout the year. Purchases increase the Inventory account balance; cost of goods sold decreases the balance.

The reasons for increasing or decreasing Inventory are as follows:

- Inventory is increased for:

  - purchases of merchandise from vendors

  - returns of merchandise from customers

- Inventory is decreased for:

  - cost of merchandise sold

  - cost of merchandise returned to vendors

  - vendor purchase allowances

  - vendor cash discounts taken and recorded under the gross method (explained later)

At year end, the Inventory account balance is current, assuming no inventory losses or errors, and can be transferred directly to the balance sheet. (Before making this transfer at year end, most companies also take a physical count of inventory on hand. If the physical count is higher than the balance in the account, the balance is increased. If the physical count is lower, the balance is decreased.)

Journal Entries for Inventory under the Perpetual Method

Merchandise purchases (which include the cost of freight when it is F.O.B. shipping point) increase Inventory and either decrease Cash or increase Accounts Payable. The entry is:

Inventory	xxxx	
Cash or Accounts Payable		xxxx

Merchandise sales require two entries. The *revenue* entry increases both Cash or Accounts Receivable, and Sales Revenue:

Cash or Accounts Receivable	xxxx	
Sales Revenue		xxxx

The *expense* entry increases Cost of Goods Sold (an expense account) and reduces Inventory:

Cost of Goods Sold	xxxx	
Inventory		xxxx

Note: Under the *periodic method* (explained in Section 3), no entries are made in the Inventory account during the year. Instead, merchandise purchases are entered in the Purchases account, freight-in is entered in the Freight-In account, and purchase returns, allowances, and discounts are entered in other accounts. At year end, these account balances are closed to compute Cost of Goods Sold.

PROBLEM 1: CriCo began operation in December. On December 20, it received a shipment of 2,250 items bought on account for $4 per unit, totaling $9,000. Terms are F.O.B. shipping point and CriCo paid the carrier the $600 freight cost on delivery. On December 28, CriCo sold one-third of the merchandise for $5,000 cash. How are these transactions recorded under the perpetual method?

SOLUTION 1:

<u>December 20</u>		
Inventory	9,600	
Accounts Payable		9,000
Cash		600

<u>December 28</u>

Cash	5,000	
Sales Revenue		5,000
Cost of Goods Sold[1]	3,200	
Inventory		3,200

[1] $9,600 cost of merchandise x 1/3 sold = $3,200.

Journal entries for various purchase reductions

There are three major categories of purchase reductions: purchase returns, purchase allowances, and purchase discounts.

>   **a. Purchase returns.** When your company purchases merchandise and later returns some or all of it, credit Inventory (to remove the cost of the returned goods from the Inventory account). If you paid for the merchandise, increase (debit) a receivable for the amount due from the vendor. If the goods were purchased on account but not paid for, decrease (debit) accounts payable for the amount.

>   **b. Purchase allowances.** When your company wants to return defective or damaged goods before paying for them, the seller may offer you an incentive, such as a reduced price, to keep them. This incentive is referred to as a *purchase allowance.* If your company accepts the allowance, reduce (credit) inventory, and reduce (debit) the liability (payable) account.

>   **PROBLEM 2:** On January 4, EnCo received 2,000 units of merchandise F.O.B. shipping point. The goods were bought on account at $4 per unit, with the seller prepaying the $200 freight cost. On January 18, EnCo pays the invoice, but on January 25 returns 15% of the merchandise. What entries does EnCo record under the perpetual method and on what dates?

SOLUTION 2:

<u>January 4</u>

Inventory	8,200[1]	
Accounts Payable		8,200

[1] 2,000 units x $4 per unit = $8,000 cost of merchandise + $200 freight cost = $8,200 total cost of merchandise.

January 18

Accounts Payable	8,200	
Cash		8,200

January 25

Receivable from Vendor	1,200	
Inventory		1,200[2]

[2] $8,000 purchase price of merchandise x 15% return = $1,200 cost of returned merchandise.

PROBLEM 3: On February 2, HuCo buys $6,000 of merchandise on account F.O.B. shipping point. It pays the shipper $400 cash. On February 8, HuCo is granted a $1,100 cost allowance for some damaged goods. On March 3, HuCo pays the invoice. What entries does HuCo record under the perpetual method and on what dates?

SOLUTION 3:

February 2

Inventory	6,400[1]	
Accounts Payable		6,000
Cash		400

[1] $6,000 cost of merchandise + $400 freight cost = $6,400 total cost of merchandise.

February 8

Accounts Payable	1,100	
Inventory		1,100

March 3

Accounts Payable	4,900[2]	
Cash		4,900

[2] $6,000 accounts payable – $1,100 purchase allowance = $4,900 amount due.

c. Purchase discounts. Sellers generally offer three kinds of discounts—volume, trade, and cash.

1. A *volume* (or *quantity*) *discount* is offered for the purchase of a large quantity. The buyer records the purchase for the amount actually billed (net of discount). Neither the prediscount price nor the discount is recorded separately in the ledger accounts.

2. A *trade* (or *professional*) *discount* is offered to buyers with whom the seller has a professional relationship, such as a lumber company that sells to carpenters. The buyer records the cost at the amount billed (net of discount) and does not record the original list price or the discount amount.

PROBLEM 4: Your company purchases merchandise listed at $30 per unit. Because the seller gives a 15% volume discount on purchases of 1,000 or more units, your company purchases 1,200 units on account. There are no freight costs. What entries should you record for the purchase?

SOLUTION 4:

Inventory	30,600[1]	
Accounts Payable		30,600

[1] $30 prediscount price per unit – $4.50 volume discount per unit [$30 x 15%] = $25.50 net of discount (invoice) price per unit x 1,200 units = $30,600 invoice cost.

3. A *cash discount* is often granted if payment is made within a specified period. The terms of this discount are expressed in the following order:

- discount percentage

- number of days in the discount period

- number of days in which payment is due if no discount is taken

For example, a 2/10, n/30 cash discount is a 2% cash discount if payment is received within 10 days. Otherwise, full payment is due within 30 days.

Purchases are recorded either at gross (the gross method) or at net (the net method).

RECORDING PURCHASES *GROSS* v. *NET* UNDER THE PERPETUAL METHOD

1. Recording purchases at gross. The buyer records the cost at the invoice price or *gross* amount, ignoring the availability of a cash discount. If the buyer pays within the discount period, the discount amount is recorded as a reduction in the cost of inventory. If the buyer does not take the cash discount, no further entry is needed. The journal entries are:

To record purchase

Inventory	xxxx	
Accounts Payable		xxxx

To record payment within the discount period

Accounts Payable	xxxx	
Inventory		xxxx
Cash		xxxx

To record payment after the discount period

Accounts Payable	xxxx	
Cash		xxxx

2. Recording purchases at net. The buyer records purchases *net of discount* (as though the discount were taken). For example, an invoice is received for $1,000 with a 5% discount if payment is made within 15 days. The buyer records the invoice at $950 (as though the discount were taken). The object is to record inventory purchases at the lowest price that the seller will accept.

If the buyer does not take the cash discount, the discount amount is recorded as a cost in *Purchase Discounts Lost* (not as a merchandise cost). This is an expense account that appears on the income statement. The entries are:

To record purchase

Inventory	xxxx	
Accounts Payable		xxxx

To record payment within the discount period

Accounts Payable	xxxx	
Cash		xxxx

To record payment after the discount period

Accounts Payable	xxxx	
Purchase Discounts Lost	xxxx	
Cash		xxxx

PROBLEM 5: On March 6, your company buys merchandise invoiced at $7,000 and there are no freight costs. Terms are 3/10, n/30. On March 14, you pay the invoice. On April 5, the merchandise is sold for $8,500 cash. What are the entries if your company records purchases at gross?

SOLUTION 5:

March 6

Inventory	7,000	
Accounts Payable		7,000

March 14

Accounts Payable	7,000	
Inventory		210^1
Cash		$6,790^1$

[1] $7,000 invoice cost – $210 cash discount [$7,000 x 3% discount] = $6,790 cash paid.

April 5

Cash	8,500	
Sales Revenue		8,500

Cost of Goods Sold	$6,790^2$	
Inventory		6,790

[2] $7,000 invoice cost – $210 cash discount = $6,790 cost of goods sold. Inventory is credited for the amount actually paid.

PROBLEM 5A: On March 6, your company buys merchandise invoiced at $7,000 and there are no freight costs. Terms are 3/10, n/30. On March 14, you pay the invoice. Then on April 5, the merchandise is sold for $8,500 cash. What are the entries if your company records purchases at net?

SOLUTION 5A:

March 6

Inventory	$6,790^1$	
Accounts Payable		6,790

[1] $7,000 gross cost of merchandise – $210 cash discount [$7,000 x 3% cash discount] = $6,790 net cost. When purchases are recorded at net, it is assumed that the invoice will be paid within the discount period.

March 14

Accounts Payable	6,790	
Cash		6,790

April 5

Cash	8,500	
Sales Revenue		8,500

Cost of Goods Sold	$6,790^2$	
Inventory		6,790

[2] $7,000 invoice cost – $210 cash discount = $6,790 cost of goods sold. Inventory is credited net of cash discount.

PROBLEM 6: Same purchase information as in Problem 5, but you pay on April 2. What entries do you record?

SOLUTION 6:

March 6

| Inventory | 7,000 | |
| Accounts Payable | | 7,000 |

April 2

| Accounts Payable | 7,000[1] | |
| Cash | | 7,000 |

[1] Your company did not pay the invoice within the discount period, so no entry is required for the discount amount.

April 5

| Cash | 8,500 | |
| Sales Revenue | | 8,500 |

| Cost of Goods Sold | 7,000 | |
| Inventory | | 7,000 |

Note: Inventory is credited for the amount actually paid.

PROBLEM 6A: Same purchase information as in Problem 5, but you pay on April 2. What entries do you record?

SOLUTION 6A:

March 6

| Inventory | 6,790 | |
| Accounts Payable | | 6,790 |

April 2

Accounts Payable	6,790	
Purchase Discounts Lost	210[1]	
Cash		7,000

[1] $7,000 gross cost of merchandise x 3% cash discount = $210 cash discount lost.

April 5

| Cash | 8,500 | |
| Sales Revenue | | 8,500 |

| Cost of Goods Sold | 6,790 | |
| Inventory | | 6,790 |

Note: Remember that inventory is credited for the purchase net of cash discount.

When a Customer Returns Merchandise

If a customer returns merchandise, record two entries.

The first entry records the reduction in sales by debiting the Sales contra account Sales Returns[1]; the second entry increases Inventory for the same amount by which Inventory was reduced in the original sale.

| Sales Returns | xxxx | |
| Cash or Accounts Receivable | | xxxx |

| Inventory | xxxx | |
| Cost of Goods Sold | | xxxx |

PROBLEM 7: On May 2, your company purchases merchandise for $5,000 F.O.B. destination and pays $5,000 cash on delivery. On May 11, you sell 70% of the goods for $8,000 on account, F.O.B. shipping point.

---

[1] A contra account is directly related to an asset, liability, or other account but has an opposite normal balance to that account. For example, Sales has a normal credit balance, so Sales Returns, a contra account, has a normal debit balance.

On May 20, your customer returns goods for which it was billed $800 but has not paid; these goods cost your company $350. What entries should you record for these transactions and on what dates?

SOLUTION 7:

<u>May 2</u>

Inventory	5,000	
Cash		5,000

<u>May 11</u>

Accounts Receivable	8,000	
Sales Revenue		8,000

Cost of Goods Sold	3,500[1]	
Inventory		3,500

[1] $5,000 cost of merchandise x 70% sold = $3,500 cost of goods sold.

<u>May 20</u>

Sales Returns	800	
Accounts Receivable		800

Inventory	350	
Cost of Goods Sold		350

Changes in the Inventory Account During the Year

Under the perpetual method, the balance in the Inventory account constantly changes during the year, increasing with each purchase, decreasing with each sale; increasing each time a customer returns goods, decreasing each time the company returns goods to the vendor. The amounts for both ending inventory and Cost of Goods Sold are simply the balances in the Inventory and Cost of Goods Sold accounts on the last day of the year. The following problem illustrates how this works.

PROBLEM 8: BiCo began operation in November, 20X3 and had only one inventory transaction during the month: a purchase on November 15 of 200 units of merchandise for $4 per unit.

During December 20X3, BiCo had the following merchandise transactions:

- On December 4, a purchase of 300 units at $4 each.

- On December 7, a sale of 230 units.

- On December 9, a purchase of 400 units at $4 each.

- On December 14, a purchase of 260 units at $4 each.

- On December 22, a sale of 540 units.

- On December 26, a puchase of 310 units at $4 each.

- On December 27, a sale of 280 units.

- On December 30, a purchase of 180 units at $4 each.

How do these transactions increase and decrease the Inventory account throughout December? What is BiCo's ending inventory for 20X3? What is BiCo's Cost of Goods Sold for 20X3?

SOLUTION 8: The following illustration shows how the balance in BiCo's Inventory account is increased and decreased throughout December as the company made purchases and sales of inventory.

Note that all year-end amounts and balances are available simply by looking at the December 31 figures. Under sales, you see that 1,050 units were sold during the year and that the cost of goods sold was $4,200. At year end, there are 600 units in ending inventory with a dollar value of $2,400.

	Inventory Account								
	Purchases			Sales			Balance		
Date	**Units**	**Unit Cost**	**Total Cost**	**Units**	**Unit Cost**	**Total Cost**	**Units**	**Unit Cost**	**Total Cost**
November 15	200	4	800				200	4	800
December 4	300	4	1,200				500	4	2,000
December 7				230	4	920	270	4	1,080
December 9	400	4	1,600				670	4	2,680
December 14	260	4	1,040				930	4	3,720
December 22				540	4	2,160	390	4	1,560
December 26	310	4	1,240				700	4	2,800
December 27				280	4	1,120	420	4	1,680
December 30	180	4	720				600	4	2,400
December 31 (Ending Inventory)									2,400
Cost of goods sold						4,200			
Cost of goods available for sale			6,600						
Total units	1,650			1,050			600		

Recording Inventory That Has Been Damaged or Lost

There is usually a discrepancy between the physical count of inventory taken at year end and the balance in the Inventory account; the physical count is usually lower. The shortfall, called *shrinkage,* may be the result of spoilage, theft, or poor recordkeeping. Shrinkage is recorded as an expense, and Inventory is reduced by the amount of the shrinkage with the following entry:

Inventory Shrinkage Expense	xxxx	
Inventory		xxxx

QUIZ 1   INVENTORY RECORDKEEPING USING THE PERPETUAL METHOD

Problem I.

Fill in the blanks.

1. The three primary categories of discounts offered by sellers are
_____, _____, and _____ discounts.

2. Under the perpetual method, the return of merchandise purchased on account is recorded in
the _____ _____ and _____ accounts.

3. When a company buys merchandise and the seller agrees to accept less than the invoice price because some of the goods are damaged, the buyer records this reduction as a(n) _____ _____.

4. On a purchase with terms 4/15, n/45, the cash discount on the purchase is _____% if the invoice is paid within _____ days.

5. When a physical count of year-end inventory yields a dollar amount lower than the balance in Inventory, the difference is referred to as _____.

Problem II.

On June 4, BuCo purchases 10,000 units of merchandise on account at $5 per unit F.O.B. destination which BuCo plans to pay in July. On June 12, BuCo sells 40% of the units for $75,000 cash, and on June 17, BuCo returns 800 units to its supplier. Prepare the entries under the perpetual inventory method showing the date of each entry.

Problem III.

On October 3, CoCo purchases 7,000 units on account at $6 per unit F.O.B. destination. On October 8, CoCo obtains a $2,000 purchase allowance from the supplier because some of the goods were defective. On October 22, CoCo sells 5,600 of the units for $75,000 cash. Prepare the entries under the perpetual inventory method, showing the date of each entry.

Problem IV.

On June 3, GiCo purchases merchandise on account. The goods cost $8,000 and the terms are F.O.B. destination 2/10, n/30. GiCo records purchases at gross. It pays the invoice on June 11. Prepare the entries using the perpetual inventory method showing the date of each entry.

Problem V.

On December 17, RaCo purchases merchandise for $5,000 F.O.B. destination, 3/10, n/30. Three days later, RaCo returns some of the goods for a $700 credit, and on the following day, it sells goods with an original purchase price of $1,100. RaCo records purchases at net. On January 28, it pays the balance due. Calculate the amount that will appear on RaCo's balance sheet under "Inventory" on December 31.

Problem VI.

On March 4, ViCo takes delivery of 700 units that it bought on account for $90 each F.O.B. shipping point, and pays the carrier $840 for freight. On March 11, ViCo sells 400 units for $46,000 cash. On March 24, ViCo returns 100 units to its supplier. On March 27, it sells 200 units on account for $24,000. On March 31, it pays the supplier's invoice. Prepare the entries under the perpetual method, showing the date of each entry.

QUIZ 1   Solutions and Explanations

Problem I.

1. trade (or professional), volume (or quantity), cash

2. Accounts Payable, Inventory

3. purchase allowance

4. 4%, 15

5. shrinkage

Problem II.

June 4

Inventory	$50,000^{1}$	
Accounts Payable		50,000

[1] 10,000 units purchased x $5 cost per unit = $50,000 cost of units purchased.

June 12

Cash	75,000	
Sales Revenue		75,000

Cost of Goods Sold	$20,000^{2}$	
Inventory		20,000

[2] $50,000 cost of units purchased x 40% sold = $20,000 cost of goods sold.

June 17

Accounts Payable	$4,000^{3}$	
Inventory		4,000

[3] 800 units returned x $5 cost per unit = $4,000 reduction in the Inventory account.

Problem III.

October 3

Inventory	42,000[1]	
Accounts Payable		42,000

[1] 7,000 units purchased x $6 cost per unit = $42,000 cost of units purchased.

October 8

Accounts Payable	2,000	
Inventory		2,000

October 22

Cash	75,000	
Sales Revenue		75,000

Cost of Goods Sold	32,000[2]	
Inventory		32,000

[2] $42,000 cost − $2,000 purchase allowance = $40,000 revised cost.
$40,000/7,000 units = $5.71 per unit cost (rounded).
$5.71 per unit cost x 5,600 units = $32,000 (rounded).

Problem IV.

June 3

Inventory	8,000	
Accounts Payable		8,000

June 11

Accounts Payable	8,000	
Inventory		160[1]
Cash		7,840[2]

[1] $8,000 cost of merchandise x 2% cash discount = $160 discount amount.

[2] $8,000 cost of merchandise − $160 cash discount amount = $7,840 cash paid.

Problem V.

$5,000	cost of merchandise
− 700	returned merchandise
$4,300	gross cost of merchandise
− 129[1]	cash discount
$4,171	net cost of merchandise
−1,067[2]	cost of goods sold
$3,104	ending inventory on RaCo's balance sheet

[1] $4,300 gross cost x 3% cash discount percentage = $129 cash discount amount. When purchases are recorded at net, Inventory is reduced even if the cash discount is not exercised.

[2] $1,100 gross cost x 3% cash discount percentage = $33 cash discount amount. $1,100 gross cost − $33 cash discount amount = $1,067 cost of goods sold.

Problem VI.

March 4

Inventory	63,840[1]	
Accounts Payable		63,000[1]
Cash		840[1]

[1]		
	$63,000	cost of merchandise
	+ 840	freight-in (shipping) cost
	$63,840	total cost of inventory

Note that this is $91.20 per unit: $63,840 total cost/700 = $91.20 per unit ($90 purchase cost + $1.20 shipping).

March 11

Cash	46,000	
Sales		46,000

Cost of Goods Sold	36,480[2]	
Inventory		36,480

[2] 400 units of merchandise sold x $91.20 cost per unit (see March 4 entry explanation) = $36,480.

March 24

Accounts Payable	9,000[3]	
Miscellaneous Expense	120[4]	
Inventory		9,120[5]

[3] 100 units of merchandise returned x $90 cost (the $1.20 per unit shipping is not included because ViCo paid the shipper directly and cannot get this cost back) = $9,000 reduction in accounts payable.

[4] 100 units of merchandise returned x $1.20 shipping cost per unit (this cost is being transferred to Miscellaneous Expense because it applies to items that were removed from inventory and returned to the manufacturer) = $120.

[5] 100 units returned to manufacturer x $91.20 total cost per unit (manufacturer's cost plus shipping cost as shown in the March 4 entry explanation) = $9,120

reduction in inventory.

March 27

Accounts Receivable	24,000	
Sales		24,000

Cost of Goods Sold	18,240[6]	
Inventory		18,240

[6] 200 units of merchandise sold x $91.20 total cost per unit = $18,240 cost of goods sold.

March 31

Accounts Payable	54,000[7]	
Cash		54,000

[7] $63,000 purchase cost owed to supplier (see March 4 entry) – $9,000 reduction in Accounts Payable (see March 24 entry) = $54,000 payment in full.

QUIZ 2   INVENTORY RECORDKEEPING USING THE PERPETUAL METHOD

Problem I.

On March 3, MiCo accepts delivery of 1,000 units F.O.B. shipping point that it purchased on account for $20 each less a 30% volume discount. The seller prepaid the $400 freight cost. On March 28, MiCo pays the amount due. Show MiCo's journal entries under the perpetual method and the dates on which they are recorded.

Problem II.

On June 12, PoCo receives $5,000 in merchandise F.O.B. destination. The company pays cash on delivery. On June 15, PoCo is granted a $900 purchase allowance because some of the goods are defective. On June 29, PoCo sells all the merchandise on account for $7,200. Record PoCo's accounting entries under the perpetual method, showing the date of each one.

Problem III.

On July 3, YaCo receives a $6,000 shipment that it bought on account, 4/10, n/45; there are no transportation costs. YaCo records purchases at net. On July 7, YaCo returns merchandise that cost $1,000. On July 11, YaCo pays the invoice. Record each journal entry under the perpetual method and the date it was made.

Problem IV.

On November 4, LuCo receives a $14,000 shipment that it bought on account, 2/15, n/60; there are no transportation costs. LuCo records purchases at gross. On November 18, LuCo pays for the goods, and on November 30 LuCo sells all the merchandise for $17,000 cash. Record LuCo's journal entries under the perpetual method, showing the date of each entry.

Problem V.

On February 11, ZoCo receives a shipment F.O.B. destination, for which it pays $15,000 cash. On February 17, ZoCo makes a $10,000 sale on account of goods that cost $6,000. On February 20, ZoCo's customer returns some of the merchandise, and ZoCo issues a $2,000 credit. Show each of ZoCo's journal entries under the perpetual method and the date of each one.

Problem VI.

On July 8, TeCo, which records purchases at net, receives 1,000 units F.O.B. shipping point that it bought on account for $60.00 each, 2/10, n/30. Upon delivery, TeCo pays the trucker $700 cash. On July 17, TeCo pays the manufacturer $58,800. On July 20, TeCo sells 600 units for $54,000 cash but on July 28 must accept a return of 50 units from a customer for an immediate cash refund. Prepare TeCo's entries for these transactions under the perpetual method and show the date of each.

QUIZ 2   Solutions and Explanations

Problem I.

March 3

Inventory	14,400[1]	
Accounts Payable		14,400

[1] $20 gross cost per unit x 30% discount = $6 discount amount.
$20 gross cost per unit – $6 discount = $14 net cost per unit.
1,000 units x $14 net cost per unit = $14,000 cost of merchandise.
$14,000 cost of merchandise + $400 prepaid freight = $14,400 total cost of merchandise.

March 28

Accounts Payable	14,400	
Cash		14,400

Problem II.

June 12

Inventory	5,000	
Cash		5,000

June 15

Receivable from Supplier	900	
Inventory		900

June 29

Accounts Receivable	7,200	
Sales Revenue		7,200

Cost of Goods Sold	4,100[1]	
Inventory		4,100

[1] $5,000 cost of merchandise – $900 purchase allowance = $4,100 net cost of merchandise.

Problem III.

<u>July 3</u>

Inventory	5,760[1]	
Accounts Payable		5,760

[1] $6,000 gross cost x 4% discount = $240 discount amount.
$6,000 gross cost – $240 discount amount = $5,760 net cost of merchandise.

<u>July 7</u>

Accounts Payable	960[2]	
Inventory		960

[2] $1,000 gross cost x 4% discount = $40 discount amount.
$1,000 gross cost of merchandise returned – $40 discount [$1,000 x 4% discount]
= $960 net cost of merchandise returned.

<u>July 11</u>

Accounts Payable	4,800[3]	
Cash		4,800

[3] $5,760 net cost of merchandise – $960 net cost of returned goods = $4,800 final
net cost of merchandise.

Problem IV.

<u>November 4</u>

Inventory	14,000	
Accounts Payable		14,000

<u>November 18</u>

Accounts Payable	14,000	
Inventory		280[1]
Cash		13,720[1]

[1] $14,000 gross cost – $280 discount [$14,000 gross cost x 2% discount] = $13,720
cash paid.

<u>November 30</u>

Cash	17,000	
Sales Revenue		17,000

Cost of Goods Sold	13,720	
Inventory		13,720[2]

[2] $14,000 gross cost – $280 discount = $13,720 net cost of goods sold.

Problem V.

February 11
Inventory   15,000
    Cash   15,000

February 17
Accounts Receivable   10,000
    Sales Revenue   10,000

Cost of Goods Sold   6,000
    Inventory   6,000

February 20
Sales Returns   2,000
    Accounts Receivable   2,000

Inventory   1,200[1]
    Cost of Goods Sold   1,200

[1] $2,000 sales return/$10,000 sales revenue = 20% of the goods returned.
$6,000 cost of goods sold x 20% of goods returned = $1,200 cost of goods
returned.

Problem VI.

July 8
Inventory   59,500[1]
    Accounts Payable   58,800
    Cash   700

[1] $60,000 purchase cost – $1,200 cash discount [$60,000 x 2%] = $58,800 net
purchase cost. $58,800 net purchase cost + $700 freight = $59,500 total purchase
cost.

July 17
Accounts Payable   58,800
    Cash   58,800

July 20
Cash   54,000
   Sales   54,000

Cost of Goods Sold   35,700[2]
   Inventory   35,700

[2] $59,500 total purchase cost/1,000 units = $59.50 per unit.
600 units sold x $59.50 total cost per unit = $35,700 cost of goods sold.

July 28
Sales Returns   4,500[3]
   Cash   4,500

[3] $54,000 sales revenue/600 units = $90 sales price per unit.
50 units returned x $90 sales price per unit = $4,500 sales returns.

Inventory   2,975[4]
   Cost of Goods Sold   2,975[4]

[4] 50 units returned x $59.50 total cost per unit = $2,975 added back to inventory
and subtracted from Cost of Goods Sold.

Section 3

INVENTORY RECORDKEEPING USING THE PERIODIC METHOD

Introduction

When a company uses the *periodic method* to maintain its inventory records, the Inventory account is not active, which means that the account is not used to record purchases or sales of inventory during the year. Instead, merchandise purchases are recorded in the Purchases account, shipping costs (F.O.B. shipping point) are recorded in the Freight-In account, and purchases returns, allowances, and discounts are recorded in other accounts.

The Inventory account is active only at year end when an adjusting entry is made to Inventory to adjust the ending balance.

(Under the *perpetual method*, each purchase and sale of inventory, including freight, is entered directly into the Inventory account throughout the year.)

Journal Entries for Inventory under the Periodic Method

The entry for merchandise purchases that include the cost of freight is:

Purchases	xxxx	
Freight-In	xxxx	
Cash or Accounts Payable		xxxx

The entry to record a merchandise purchase when the company pays the shipper directly is:

Purchases	xxxx	
Cash or Accounts Payable		xxxx
Freight-In	xxxx	
Cash		xxxx

The entry to record a merchandise sale increases Cash or Accounts Receivable and also increases Sales Revenue. It is recorded as follows:

Cash or Accounts Receivable	xxxx	
Sales Revenue		xxxx

Journal entries for various purchase reductions

There are three general categories of purchase reductions: purchase returns, purchase allowances, and purchase discounts. These reductions are not credited to Purchases, but instead are credited to Purchases *contra accounts.*[1]

a. Purchase returns. When your company purchases merchandise, then returns some or all of it:

- Credit the cost of the returned goods to Purchase Returns. This is a Purchases contra account and therefore has a normal credit balance (because Purchases, the account to which it is related, has a normal debit balance).

- Debit either a receivable or a payable as follows:

If your company has paid for the merchandise, record a receivable for the amount due from the vendor:

Receivable from Supplier	xxxx	
Purchase Returns		xxxx

If your company purchased the goods on account and has not paid for them, record a reduction in Accounts Payable:

Accounts Payable	xxxx	
Purchase Returns		xxxx

b. Purchase allowances. When your company is granted a purchase allowance (a reduction in cost), record the amount in Purchase Allowances (another contra account to Purchases).

Accounts Payable	xxxx	
Purchase Allowances		xxxx

Some companies use one contra account for both returns and allowances, the Purchase Returns and Allowances account.

---

[1] A contra account is directly related to an asset, liability, or other account, but it has an opposite normal balance to that account. For example, Purchases has a normal debit balance, so Purchases contra accounts have a normal credit balance.

PROBLEM 1: On March 11, your company purchases merchandise for $13,000 on account F.O.B. shipping point, and it pays the $700 freight bill on delivery. On March 15, your company returns 20% of the goods to the seller. On March 17, your company pays the amount due. On March 29, your company sells the goods for $24,000 cash. What entries do you record and on what dates?

SOLUTION 1:

March 11

Purchases	13,000	
Accounts Payable		13,000

Freight-In	700	
Cash		700

March 15

Accounts Payable	2,600	
Purchase Returns		2,600[1]

[1] $13,000 cost of merchandise x 20% merchandise returned = $2,600 cost of returned merchandise.

March 17

Accounts Payable	10,400[2]	
Cash		10,400

[2] $13,000 cost of merchandise − $2,600 cost of returned merchandise = $10,400 due.

March 29*

Cash	24,000	
Sales Revenue		24,000

* Under the periodic method, the Inventory and Cost of Goods Sold accounts are adjusted at the end of the period, not when a sale is made.

PROBLEM 2: On December 2, your company buys merchandise for $20,000 on account F.O.B. shipping point; the seller prepays the $600 shipping charge. Because some of the goods were damaged, on December 8, you are granted a $1,500 cost allowance. On December 13, you sell the goods for $31,000 on account, and on December 23 you pay the supplier the amount due. What entries does your company record for these transactions and on what dates?

SOLUTION 2:

<u>December 2</u>

Purchases	20,000	
Freight-In	600	
Accounts Payable		20,600[1]

[1] $20,000 cost of merchandise + $600 freight = $20,600 total due seller.

<u>December 8</u>

Accounts Payable	1,500	
Purchase Allowances		1,500

<u>December 13</u>

Accounts Receivable	31,000	
Sales Revenue		31,000

<u>December 23</u>

Accounts Payable	19,100[2]	
Cash		19,100

[2] $20,600 original amount due – $1,500 purchase allowance = $19,100 paid.

c. Purchase discounts. Many vendors offer a *volume* (or *quantity*) *discount* for the purchase of a large quantity, and a *trade* (or *professional*) *discount* to buyers with whom the seller has a professional relationship, such as a paper supplier that sells to printers. Buyers record both kinds of discounts for the amount actually billed (net of discount); the original list price and the discount amount are not recorded.

PROBLEM 3: Your company buys units listed at $80 each. To take advantage of a 10% volume discount on purchases of 700 units or more, your company buys 1,000 units on account. The seller pays the freight. What is the entry to record this purchase?

SOLUTION 3:

Purchases	72,000[1]	
Accounts Payable		72,000

[1] $80 list price per unit x 10% volume discount = $8 discount per unit. $80 list price – $8 discount = $72 net-of-discount price per unit. 1,000 units purchased x $72 net-of-discount price per unit = $72,000 invoice cost.

Sellers may offer *cash discounts* for payment within a specified period. The terms of these discounts, as noted in Section 2, are expressed in an abbreviated format in the following order:

- discount percentage;
- number of days in the discount period; and
- number of days after which the payment is overdue.

For example, a 3/15, n/45 cash discount is a 3% cash discount if payment is received within 15 days. Otherwise, full payment is due within 45 days.

Buyers that use the periodic method may account for cash discounts in two ways: at gross or at net (just like buyers that use the perpetual method).

RECORDING PURCHASES *GROSS* V. *NET* UNDER THE PERIODIC METHOD

1. Recording purchases at gross. The buyer records the invoice price as though no cash discount were offered. If the buyer takes the discount, the discount amount is recorded in the contra account Purchase Discounts; if no discount is taken, no entry is needed.

To record purchase
| Purchases | xxxx | |
| Accounts Payable | | xxxx |

To record payment within the discount period
Accounts Payable	xxxx	
Purchase Discounts		xxxx
Cash		xxxx

To record payment after the discount period
| Accounts Payable | xxxx | |
| Cash | | xxxx |

2. Recording purchases at net. The buyer records the discounted price as though the discount had been taken. If the buyer does not pay within the discount period, the additional amount paid for the lost discount is recorded in the account Purchase Discounts Lost (an expense account).

To record purchase
| Purchases | xxxx | |
| Accounts Payable | | xxxx |

To record payment within the discount period
| Accounts Payable | xxxx | |
| Cash | | xxxx |

To record payment after the discount period
Accounts Payable	xxxx	
Purchase Discounts Lost	xxxx	
Cash		xxxx

PROBLEM 4: On July 6, your company buys merchandise listed at $17,000. Terms are 3/10, n/30 and the seller pays the freight. On July 14, you pay the invoice. On August 5, your company sells the merchandise for $28,500 cash. If purchases are recorded at gross, what are the entries?

SOLUTION 4:

July 6
| Purchases | 17,000 | |
| Accounts Payable | | 17,000 |

July 14
Accounts Payable	17,000	
Purchase Discounts		510[1]
Cash		16,490[1]

[1] $17,000 invoice cost – $510 discount [$17,000 cost x 3% discount] = $16,490 paid.

August 5
| Cash | 28,500 | |
| Sales Revenue | | 28,500 |

PROBLEM 4A: On July 6, your company buys merchandise listed at $17,000. Terms are 3/10, n/30, and the seller pays the freight. On July 14, you pay the invoice, and on August 5, your company sells the merchandise for $28,500 cash. If purchases are recorded at net, what are the entries?

SOLUTION 4A:

July 6
| Purchases | 16,490[1] | |
| Accounts Payable | | 16,490 |

[1] $17,000 cost of merchandise – $510 discount [$17,000 cost x 3% discount] = $16,490 cost net of cash discount.

July 14
| Accounts Payable | 16,490 | |
| Cash | | 16,490 |

August 5
| Cash | 28,500 | |
| Sales Revenue | | 28,500 |

PROBLEM 5: Using the purchase data in Problem 4, assume that you pay the invoice on August 2. If you record purchases at gross, what entries do you record?

SOLUTION 5:

July 6
Purchases	17,000	
Accounts Payable		17,000

August 2
Accounts Payable	17,000	
Cash		17,000

August 5
Cash	28,500	
Sales Revenue		28,500

PROBLEM 5A: Using the purchase information in Problem 4A, assume that you pay the invoice on August 2. If you record purchases at net, what entries do you record?

SOLUTION 5A:

July 6
Purchases	16,490[1]	
Accounts Payable		16,490

[1] $17,000 cost of merchandise − $510 discount [$17,000 cost x 3% discount] = $16,490 cost net of cash discount.

August 2
Accounts Payable	16,490	
Purchase Discounts Lost	510[2]	
Cash		17,000

[2] $17,000 cost of merchandise x 3% discount = $510 cash discount lost.

August 5
Cash	28,500	
Sales Revenue		28,500

When a Customer Returns Merchandise

If a customer returns merchandise, record the amount in Sales Returns, a contra account to Sales (*not* in Inventory or Cost of Goods Sold).

Sales Returns	xxxx	
Cash or Accounts Receivable		xxxx

PROBLEM 6: On March 12, your company purchases merchandise for $15,000 F.O.B. destination and pays cash on delivery. On March 21, you sell 60% of these goods on account for $28,000 F.O.B. shipping point. On March 28, you receive a return of goods that you sold for $5,600 and that cost your company $3,000. What entries do you record for these transactions and on what dates?

SOLUTION 6:

March 12
Purchases	15,000	
Cash		15,000

March 21
Accounts Receivable	28,000	
Sales Revenue		28,000

<u>March 28</u>
Sales Returns   5,600
    Accounts Receivable   5,600

Year-end Adjustments under the Periodic Method

Because the Inventory account is not used during the year under the periodic method, the balance on December 31 (ending balance) is the same on January 1 (beginning balance). This beginning balance is transferred to the *unadjusted* trial balance at year end along with the following items:

- *merchandise costs* for the period recorded in Purchases;

- *transportation costs* recorded in Freight-In;

- *discounts on merchandise which the company has received* that have been recorded in Purchase Discounts;

- *merchandise for which the company received an allowance* which is recorded in the contra account Purchase Allowances, and *merchandise the company returned* which is recorded in the contra account Purchase Returns (or Purchase Returns and Allowances).

To determine *ending inventory,* which is the Inventory account balance as of December 31, a physical count of inventory is required.

Net Inventory Purchased for the Year

The net purchases computation is as follows:

Gross purchases of inventory
–   Purchase reductions*
Subtotal
+   Freight-In
Net purchases of inventory

* Purchase Returns balance + Purchase Allowances balance + Purchases Discounts balance.

Important: If purchases are recorded under the gross method, only discounts *actually taken* are subtracted from gross purchases as purchase reductions. If purchases are recorded under the net method, 100% of discounts *offered* are omitted from gross purchases. The portion of discounts not taken is recorded in Purchase Discounts Lost, an expense account, and is reported as a general business expense unrelated to inventory.

The Cost of Goods Sold (COGS)
Computation at Year End

Under the periodic method, COGS must be computed at year end. This year-end schedule (computation) is presented on the income statement or on a *cost of goods sold schedule*:

Cost of goods sold schedule (or "cost of goods sold statement"):

Beginning inventory
<u>+   Net purchases</u>
Cost of goods available for sale
<u>–   Ending inventory</u>
Cost of goods sold

Note: These calculations are not needed under the *perpetual* method because purchase costs and deductions are recorded directly in the Inventory account at each purchase, and the cost of goods sold is recorded at each sale.

PROBLEM 7: Your company's ending inventory is $48,000, and the previous year's ending inventory was $43,000. Merchandise purchases for the current year are $475,000, and freight-in costs are $11,000. There are $2,000 in cash discounts (your company records purchases at gross). $15,000 of merchandise was returned, and your company received $3,000 in cost allowances for defective items. Show the calculations to derive cost of goods sold.

SOLUTION 7: Before you can compute cost of goods sold, compute net purchases:

$475,000	gross purchases
– 20,000*	purchase reductions
$455,000	subtotal
+ 11,000	freight-in
$466,000	net purchases

* $15,000 purchase returns + $3,000 purchase allowances + $2,000 purchase discounts = $20,000 purchase reductions.

Now you can show the cost of goods sold schedule:

$ 43,000	beginning inventory (same as last year's ending inventory)
+466,000	net purchases
$509,000	cost of goods available for sale
– 48,000	ending inventory
$461,000	cost of goods sold

Even though the COGS components appear on some income statements, most businesses compute COGS by recording a single adjusting entry in the general journal. The entry adjusts the Inventory account and closes out all merchandise inventory-related accounts to the Cost of Goods Sold account. In the entry, cost of goods sold is the "balancing amount" because the amount is computed ("plugged"):

Ending Inventory	xxxx	
Purchase Returns	xxxx	
Purchase Allowances	xxxx	
Purchase Discounts	xxxx	
Cost of Goods Sold [balancing amount]	xxxx	
Purchases		xxxx
Freight-In		xxxx
Beginning Inventory		xxxx

Note that this entry is really the COGS computation above turned upside down.

The COGS entry	**The COGS computation**
Ending Inventory	**Beginning inventory**
Purchase Returns	
Purchase Allowances	
Purchase Discounts	**+ Net purchases**
Cost of Goods Sold	
[balancing amount]	
Purchases	
Freight-In	
Beginning Inventory	**– Ending inventory**
	= Cost of goods sold

Important: In most cases, accountants do not debit Ending Inventory and credit Beginning Inventory. Instead, they use Inventory in the entry just once as either a net debit (if ending inventory is greater than beginning inventory) or a net credit (if ending inventory is less than beginning inventory). The reason is that accounting personnel usually net the Inventory account before recording the adjusting entry above.

The closing entry above accomplishes three very important goals:

1. The entry closes out the Purchases and Freight-In accounts with a credit (both accounts have normal debit balances) and closes all Purchases contra accounts with a debit (because Purchase Returns, Purchase Allowances and Purchase Discounts have normal credit balances).

2. The entry is used to compute cost of goods sold. All debits are credited, and all credits are debited. The difference between total debits and total credits becomes COGS. This difference is known as the balancing or "plug" amount.

3. The entry adjusts the beginning inventory balance in the Inventory account to arrive at ending inventory for the year (which will be beginning inventory for next year). Inventory (that is, *beginning* inventory) is adjusted up or down depending on the physical count of ending inventory.

PROBLEM 8: Using the data in Problem 7, prepare the year-end adjusting entry to adjust Inventory, close out all inventory-related accounts and compute Cost of Goods Sold:

SOLUTION 8: The entry is:

Ending Inventory	48,000	
Purchase Returns	15,000	
Purchase Allowances	3,000	
Purchase Discounts	2,000	
Cost of Goods Sold	?	
Purchases		475,000
Freight-In		11,000
Beginning Inventory		43,000

To calculate the cost of goods sold amount:

529,000	total credits
− 68,000	total debits
461,000	cost of goods sold

Thus, the complete closing entry is:

Ending Inventory	48,000	
Purchase Returns	15,000	
Purchase Allowances	3,000	
Purchase Discounts	2,000	
Cost of Goods Sold	**461,000**	
Purchases		475,000
Freight-In		11,000
Beginning Inventory		43,000

This entry is really the COGS computation above turned upside down.

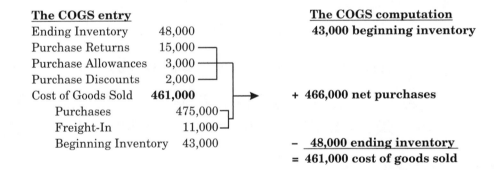

The COGS entry		The COGS computation
Ending Inventory	48,000	**43,000 beginning inventory**
Purchase Returns	15,000	
Purchase Allowances	3,000	
Purchase Discounts	2,000	
Cost of Goods Sold	**461,000**	**+ 466,000 net purchases**
Purchases	475,000	
Freight-In	11,000	
Beginning Inventory	43,000	**− 48,000 ending inventory**
		= 461,000 cost of goods sold

Summary

The periodic method of inventory recordkeeping does not use the Inventory account during the year. Purchases are recorded in the Purchases account and other costs such as freight or deductions, like returns, allowances, and discounts, are recorded in Purchases contra accounts. At year end, a single adjusting entry is used to close out Purchases and its contra accounts to derive the cost of goods sold and to adjust the Inventory account so that the closing balance is ending (rather than beginning) inventory.

QUIZ 1 INVENTORY RECORDKEEPING USING THE PERIODIC METHOD

Problem I.

On July 7, DiCo purchases merchandise on account for $32,000 F.O.B. shipping point; the seller prepays the $400 shipping cost. DiCo uses the periodic method. On July 11, DiCo is granted a $2,200 cost allowance because the goods do not meet its specifications. On July 31, DiCo pays the amount due. Prepare the entries DiCo makes, up to and including final payment of the seller's invoice, and show the date of each entry.

Problem II.

During its first year in business, RoCo, which uses the periodic method, purchases merchandise for $678,000 and incurs no freight costs. It returns goods costing $6,000 and is granted cost allowances of $2,000. RoCo, which records purchases at gross, was offered $5,100 of cash discounts, but took only $3,300. At year end, RoCo takes a physical count of its inventory and finds $67,900 in goods on hand.

1. Calculate RoCo's cost of goods sold using the COGS schedule.

2. Give the adjusting journal entry to adjust Inventory, and close out all inventory-related accounts to Cost of Goods Sold.

Problem III.

On May 5, NiCo purchases 10,000 units of merchandise on account F.O.B. destination. NiCo uses the periodic method. Although the purchased merchandise has an invoice cost of $6 per unit, NiCo gets a 15% trade discount and the seller will absorb the $700 freight charge, although NiCo will have to lay out the cash. On May 9, NiCo returns 300 units. On May 18, NiCo sells the entire shipment for $66,000 cash, and on May 24, it pays the vendor's invoice. Prepare all of NiCo's entries, and show the date of each.

Problem IV.

VuCo had merchandise on hand at the end of last year that had cost $54,000; at the end of the current year, the value of the goods on hand is $47,000. VuCo uses the periodic method. During the year purchases were $777,000, transportation costs totaled $21,100, and purchase returns were $18,000. Purchase allowances were $3,000, and cash discounts exercised totaled $11,500. VuCo records purchases at gross. Give the year-end entry to adjust Inventory, and close out all merchandise inventory-related accounts to Cost of Goods Sold.

Problem V.

On March 17, YeCo purchases 8,000 items on account at a cost of $16,000 F.O.B. shipping point, and it pays the $600 transportation cost when the goods are delivered. YeCo uses the periodic method. On March 25, YeCo sells 6,500 items on account for $4 each, for a total sale of $26,000. On March 28, the customer returns 1,625 items to YeCo as defective, and YeCo in turn sends the merchandise back to its supplier the next day. On March 31, YeCo pays the amount due. Prepare the accounting entries, rounding all amounts to the nearest dollar, and show the date of each entry.

QUIZ 1   *Solutions and Explanations*

Problem I.

July 7

Purchases	32,000	
Freight-In	400	
Accounts Payable		32,400[1]

[1] $32,000 cost of merchandise + $400 freight prepaid by seller = $32,400 due to seller.

July 11

Accounts Payable	2,200	
Purchase Allowances		2,200

July 31

Accounts Payable	30,200[2]	
Cash		30,200

[2] $32,400 original amount due − $2,200 purchase allowance = $30,200 paid.

Problem II.

1. RoCo's cost of goods sold can be computed in two steps:

Computation #1. Calculating net inventory purchased during the year:

$678,000	gross purchases
− 11,300*	purchase reductions
$666,700	subtotal
+ 0	freight-in
$666,700	net purchases

* $6,000 purchase returns + $2,000 purchase allowances + $3,300 purchase discounts = $11,300 purchase reductions.

Computation #2. Calculating the cost of goods sold for the year:

$	0	beginning inventory
	+666,700	net purchases of inventory
$666,700		goods available for sale
	− 67,900	ending inventory
$598,800		cost of goods sold

The entry to adjust Inventory and close out all inventory-related accounts to Cost of Goods Sold is:

Ending Inventory	67,900
Purchase Returns	6,000
Purchase Allowances	2,000
Purchase Discounts	3,300[1]
Cost of Goods Sold	?
Purchases	678,000
Freight-In[2]	0
Beginning Inventory[2]	0

[1] Only the $3,300 discount exercised needs to appear in the entry because the company records purchases at gross. The portion of discounts not taken was never recorded, so no adjustment for this amount is required.

[2] These two accounts are included in the entry for teaching purposes only; they would not appear in an actual entry. Beginning Inventory has a zero balance because it is the company's first year of business.

To derive cost of goods sold:

$678,000	total credits
− 79,200	total debits
$598,800	cost of goods sold

The closing entry, showing COGS as the balancing amount, is:

Ending Inventory	67,900
Purchase Returns	6,000
Purchase Allowances	2,000
Purchase Discounts	3,300
Cost of Goods Sold	**598,800**
Purchases	678,000
Freight-In*	0
Beginning Inventory*	0

* These two accounts are included in the entry for teaching purposes only; they would not appear in an actual entry. Beginning Inventory has a zero balance because it is the company's first year of business.

This entry is really the COGS computation shown earlier and now turned upside down.

The COGS entry

Ending Inventory	67,900
Purchase Returns	6,000
Purchase Allowances	2,000
Purchase Discounts	3,300
Cost of Goods Sold	598,800
Purchases	678,000
Freight-In	0
Beginning Inventory	0

The COGS computation

0 beginning inventory

+ 666,700 net purchases

–   67,900 ending inventory

= 598,800 cost of goods sold

Problem III.

May 5

Purchases	51,000[1]
Cash	700
Accounts Payable	50,300[2]

[1] $6 invoice cost per unit – $0.90 discount per unit ($6 x 15% discount) = $5.10 actual cost per unit.
10,000 units purchased x $5.10 cost per unit = $51,000 cost of purchase.

[2] $51,000 cost of merchandise – $700 freight paid directly to shipper on behalf of seller = $50,300 due to seller.

May 9

Accounts Payable	1,530[3]	
Purchase Returns		1,530

[3] 300 units returned x $5.10 invoice cost per unit = $1,530 reduction in amount due seller.

May 18

Cash	66,000	
Sales Revenue		66,000

May 24

Accounts Payable	48,770[4]	
Cash		48,770

[4] $50,300 originally due seller – $1,530 reduction for purchase returns = $48,770 paid to seller.

Problem IV.

The entry to adjust Inventory and close out all merchandise inventory-related accounts to Cost of Goods Sold is:

Ending Inventory	47,000
Purchase Returns	18,000
Purchase Allowances	3,000
Purchase Discounts	11,500
Cost of Goods Sold	**?**
Purchases	777,000
Freight-In	21,100
Beginning Inventory	54,000

To derive cost of goods sold:

$852,100	total credits
– 79,500	total debits
$772,600	cost of goods sold

Ending Inventory	47,000	
Purchase Returns	18,000	
Purchase Allowances	3,000	
Purchase Discounts	11,500	
Cost of Goods Sold	**772,600**	
Purchases		777,000
Freight-In		21,100
Beginning Inventory		54,000

Problem V.

March 17

Purchases	16,000	
Accounts Payable		16,000
Freight-In	600	
Cash		600

March 25

Accounts Receivable	26,000	
Sales Revenue		26,000

March 28

Sales Returns	6,500[1]	
Accounts Receivable		6,500

[1] 1,625 items returned by customer x $4 per item = $6,500 total return.

March 29

Accounts Payable	3,250	
Purchase Returns		3,250[2]

[2] 1,625 items returned to vendor by YeCo x $2 per item ($16,000 cost of merchandise purchased ÷ 8,000 items purchased) = $3,250 cost of merchandise YeCo returned to vendor.

March 31

Accounts Payable	12,750[3]	
Cash		12,750

[3] $16,000 cost of merchandise – $3,250 cost of merchandise returned = $12,750 YeCo must pay its vendor.

QUIZ 2   INVENTORY RECORDKEEPING USING THE PERIODIC METHOD

Problem I.

HiCo uses the periodic method. On January 3, HiCo purchases merchandise on account for $41,000 F.O.B. destination. On January 5, HiCo returns merchandise for which it receives a $5,000 credit. On January 9, HiCo sells merchandise for $13,000 on account; this merchandise cost the company $7,000. On January 18, HiCo pays the amount due, and on January 22, HiCo's customer returns 20% of the merchandise along with its payment for the balance due. Prepare HiCo's accounting entries, and show the date of each entry.

Problem II.

GaCo uses the periodic method for inventory and records purchases at net. On March 3, it purchases merchandise for $50,000 on account, 2/10, n/30 F.O.B. destination. On March 8, it is granted a cost allowance of $4,000 for defective merchandise, and on March 12, it pays the amount due. Prepare GaCo's accounting entries, and show the date of each entry.

Problem III.

On November 3, BuCo, which uses the periodic method, purchases merchandise on account for $82,000. There are no freight costs, and terms are 3/15, n/45. BuCo record purchases at net. On November 14, BuCo returns merchandise with an invoice cost of $10,000, and on November 27, BuCo pays the amount due. Prepare BuCo's accounting entries, and show the date of each entry.

Problem IV.

On February 4, YoCo purchases 1,200 cases of merchandise on account. The invoice cost is $40 a case, but if more than 500 cases are purchased there is a 15% volume discount. Terms are F.O.B. shipping point and the seller prepays the $900 transportation cost. YoCo returns 20 cases on February 11 and pays the amount due on February 28. YoCo uses the periodic method of inventory recordkeeping. Prepare YoCo's accounting entries.

Problem V.

In 20X3, WiCo's ending inventory was $45,000, and in 20X4 it was $38,000. WiCo's 20X4 purchases totaled $120,000. WiCo was offered $2,000 in cash discounts, but exercised only $500 of these. Transportation-in was $5,500. WiCo uses the periodic method for inventory and records purchases at net. Prepare the cost of goods sold schedule.

QUIZ 2 Solutions and Explanations

Problem I.

<u>January 3</u>
Purchases   41,000
    Accounts Payable   41,000

<u>January 5</u>
Accounts Payable   5,000
    Purchase Returns   5,000

<u>January 9</u>
Accounts Receivable   13,000
    Sales Revenue   13,000

<u>January 18</u>
Accounts Payable   36,000[1]
    Cash   36,000

[1] $41,000 cost of merchandise – $5,000 cost of merchandise returned = $36,000 payment due.

<u>January 22</u>
Sales Returns   2,600[2]
Cash   10,400[3]
    Accounts Receivable   13,000

[2] $13,000 sales revenue x 20% merchandise returned = $2,600 sales returns.

[3] $13,000 sales revenue – $2,600 sales returns = $10,400 collected.

Problem II.

March 3

Purchases	49,000[1]
Accounts Payable	49,000

[1] $50,000 invoice cost of merchandise x 2% discount = $1,000 cash discount. $50,000 invoice cost of merchandise – $1,000 cash discount = $49,000 net purchase cost.

March 8

Accounts Payable	3,920[2]
Purchase Allowances	3,920

[2] $4,000 invoice cost of merchandise on which cost allowance was granted x 2% cash discount = $80 cash discount available.
$4,000 invoice cost of merchandise for which cost allowance was granted – $80 cash discount available = $3,920 net cost.

March 12

Accounts Payable	45,080[3]
Cash	45,080

[3] $49,000 net purchase cost – $3,920 purchase allowance (at net cost) = $45,080 due.

Problem III.

November 3

Purchases	79,540[1]
Accounts Payable	79,540

[1] $82,000 invoice cost of merchandise x 3% cash discount = $2,460 cash discount available.
$82,000 invoice cost of merchandise – $2,460 cash discount available = $79,540 net purchase cost.

November 14

Accounts Payable	9,700[2]
Purchase Returns	9,700

[2] $10,000 invoice cost of returned merchandise x 3% discount = $300 discount available on returned merchandise.
$10,000 invoice cost of returned merchandise – $300 discount not taken = $9,700 net cost of returned merchandise.

<u>November 27</u>

Accounts Payable	69,840[3]	
Purchase Discounts Lost	2,160[4]	
Cash		72,000[5]

[3] $79,540 net purchase cost – $9,700 purchase return (at net) = $69,840 net cost.

[4] $2,460 discount lost – $300 cash discount on returned merchandise = $2,160 total cash discount lost.

[5] $82,000 gross cost of merchandise – $10,000 merchandise returned (at gross) = $72,000 gross cost of merchandise.

Problem IV.

<u>February 4</u>

Purchases	40,800[1]	
Freight-In	900	
Accounts Payable		41,700[2]

[1] $40 prediscount cost per unit x 15% volume discount = $6 discount per unit.
$40 prediscount cost per unit – $6 volume discount per unit = $34 net cost per unit.
1,200 units purchased x $34 net cost per unit = $40,800 cost of purchase.

[2] $40,800 cost of merchandise + $900 freight paid by seller = $41,700 due.

<u>February 11</u>

Accounts Payable	680[3]	
Purchase Returns		680

[3] 20 units returned x $34 net cost per unit = $680 cost of returned merchandise.

<u>February 28</u>

Accounts Payable	41,020[4]	
Cash		41,020

[4] $41,700 original amount due – $680 cost of returned merchandise = $41,020 amount paid.

Problem V.

To compute net purchases:

$120,000 gross purchases
−   2,000* purchase reductions
$118,000 subtotal
+   5,500 freight-in
$123,500 net purchases

* Because merchandise purchases were recorded under the net method, the entire discount is subtracted from gross purchases when computing net purchases. Any portion of the discount not taken will be recorded in Purchase Discounts Lost, an expense account, and will be reported as a general business expense unrelated to inventory. (See page 39.)

To compute cost of goods sold:

$ 45,000 beginning inventory (same as last year's ending inventory)
+123,500 net purchases
$168,500 cost of goods available for sale
− 38,000 ending inventory
$130,500 cost of goods sold

INVENTORY COSTING: THE WEIGHTED-AVERAGE AND MOVING-AVERAGE METHODS

Introduction

When a company purchases merchandise, it is simply recorded at cost. However, when the company sells the merchandise, there is no easy way to know the cost of the particular items sold.

For example, a beverage distributor may make hundreds of purchases involving thousands of cases, with each purchase at a slightly different price. The distributor can easily record the cost of each purchase when the shipment arrives. But when the distributor makes a sale, how can it determine the cost of the particular cases sold (cost of goods sold or COGS)—or the cost of the particular cases on hand at year end (ending inventory)?*

A company must compute the cost of goods sold for its income statement (under expenses) and the cost of ending inventory for its balance sheet (under assets).

To compute ending inventory and COGS, companies select one of three *costing methods:*

1. Weighted-average (if the periodic method is used) and moving [weighted] average (if the perpetual method is used);

2. First-in-first-out (FIFO);

3. Last-in-first-out (LIFO).

This section covers weighted-average costing under the periodic method and moving-average costing under the perpetual method.

---

*A very few industries can measure inventory cost easily with the *specific identification method,* which uses the precise cost of each piece of merchandise sold. For example, an auto dealer knows the cost of each car it sells by the car's serial number. Jewelers keep records of the cost of each diamond, gold necklace, etc., that they sell. Both auto dealers and jewelers also know the precise cost of inventory on hand at year end.

Note: Depending on how you compute a weighted or moving average, rounding can result in substantially different answers. For example, if a computation is done in several steps, rounding each step to dollars or to cents will result in a very different answer than if each step uses 8 or 9 decimal places and rounding takes place only in the last step. Generally, you can tell if your answer is off because of rounding or an error.

How to Use Weighted-Average Costing Under the Periodic Method

The first step in any costing method is to find the cost per unit. Using a *weighted average* ensures a more accurate cost than using a *simple average*, as the following example shows.

EXAMPLE 1: TiCo buys 10 items in January at $4 each, 6 items in February at $7 each, and 223 items in March at $3 each. What is TiCo's cost per unit using *weighted-average* costing?

To compute:

10	items in January x $4 per unit	= $ 40 January purchase cost
6	items in February x $7 per unit =	42 February purchase cost
+223	items in March x $3 per unit	= +669 March purchase cost
239	total items	= $751 total purchase cost

$$\frac{\$751 \text{ total purchase cost}}{239 \text{ total units}} = \$3.14 \text{ weighted - average cost per unit}$$

You cannot use a *simple average*, because it gives you the wrong answer:

$4 per unit (January) + $7 per unit (February) + $3 per unit (March)
= $14 cost of units using a *simple average*

$$\frac{\$14 \text{ unit cost total}}{3 \text{ purchases}} = \$4.67 \text{ per unit simple - average cost per unit}$$

The incorrect *simple average* is 49% (rounded) higher than the correct *weighted average*.

To find the cost per unit, use the following formula:

$$\frac{\text{Cost of goods available for sale}}{\text{Units available for sale}} = \text{weighted-average cost per unit}$$

Once you know the weighted-average cost per unit, it is relatively easy to compute ending inventory and cost of goods sold. Ending inventory is computed *before* COGS, because it is used in the COGS computation.

To compute ending inventory:
Number of units on hand at year end x weighted-average cost per unit = ending inventory

To compute COGS:
Number of units sold x weighted-average cost per unit = weighted-average cost of goods sold

Using Weighted-Average Costing Beginning in a Company's First Year of Operation

To use the formula

$$\frac{\text{Cost of goods available for sale}}{\text{Units available for sale}} = \text{weighted-average cost per unit}$$

First compute *cost of goods available for sale* and *total units available for sale.*

To compute cost of goods available for sale: For a company's first year of operation, the cost of goods available for sale is the same as net purchases:

Gross purchases
− Purchase reductions*
Subtotal
+ Freight-in
Cost of goods available for sale (same as net purchases in the first year)

* Purchase returns + purchase allowances + purchase discounts.

To compute total units available for sale: For a company's first year of operation, the units available for sale are the same as net units purchased:

Gross units purchased
– Units returned
Units available for sale (same as net units purchased in the first year)

To illustrate how weighted-average costing is used, follow the example of the MiCo company in Problems 1–7.

PROBLEM 1: MiCo begins operations in 20X1. It has total purchases of 17 units at a total cost of $100 and freight-in of $14. It returns 2 units that cost $1 each, receives a purchase allowance of $1, and takes advantage of $6 in purchase discounts. What is MiCo's cost of goods available for sale for 20X1?

SOLUTION 1: *To compute MiCo's cost of goods available for sale:*

$100	total purchases
– 9*	purchase reductions
$ 91	subtotal
+ 14	freight-in
$105	cost of goods available for sale

* $2 purchase returns + $1 purchase allowances + $6 purchase discounts = $9 purchases reductions.

MiCo's cost of goods available for sale in 20X1 is $105.

PROBLEM 2: Based on the data in Problem 1, how many units does MiCo have available for sale in 20X1?

SOLUTION 2: *To compute units available for sale:*

17	gross units purchased
– 2	units returned
15	units available for sale

MiCo has 15 units available for sale in 20X1.

Note that net purchases for 20X1 are also 15 units. In a company's first year, net units purchased are the same as total units available for sale because there is no beginning inventory.

PROBLEM 3: What is MiCo's cost per unit in its first year of business under the weighted-average formula?

SOLUTION 3: The weighted-average formula is:

$$\frac{\text{Cost of goods available for sale}}{\text{Units available for sale}} = \text{weighted-average cost per unit}$$

$$\frac{\$105^* \text{ cost of goods available for sale}}{\$15^{**} \text{ units available for sale}} = \$7 \text{ weighted-average cost per unit}$$

   * See Solution 1.
 ** See Solution 2.

PROBLEM 4: A physical count of MiCo's inventory at year-end 20X1 shows 6 units still on hand. In MiCo's first year of business, what is its ending inventory? What is its COGS?

SOLUTION 4: *To compute MiCo's ending inventory for its first year of operation:*

6 units on hand at year end x $7 cost per unit = $42 ending inventory

To compute MiCo's COGS for its first year of operation:

9* units sold during the year x $7 unit cost = $63 cost of goods sold

* 15 units available for sale – 6 units in ending inventory.

To compute MiCo's COGS:

$100	gross purchases
– 9*	purchase reductions
91	net purchases
+ 14	freight-in
$105	cost of goods available for sale
– 42	ending inventory
$ 63	COGS

* $1 purchase returns + $2 purchases allowances + $6 purchase discounts = $9 purchase reductions (information supplied in Problem 2).

Computing COGS and Ending Inventory After a Company's First Year of Operation

After a company's first year of operation, each year's ending inventory becomes the following year's beginning inventory. Thus, the ending inventory for Year 1 becomes the beginning inventory for Year 2.

Here is how MiCo costs out ending inventory in its second year of business, 20X2.

PROBLEM 5: In 20X2, MiCo has beginning inventory of $42*, gross purchases of $310, purchase returns of $4, purchase allowances of $3, purchase discounts of $2, and freight-in of $7. What is MiCo's 20X2 cost of goods available for sale?

* Same as 20X1 ending inventory computed in Problem 4.

SOLUTION 5: To compute MiCo's 20X2 cost of units available for sale, first compute MiCo's 20X2 net purchases:

To compute net purchases:

$310	gross purchases
– 9*	purchase reductions
$301	subtotal
+ 7	freight-in
$308	net purchases

* $4 purchase returns + $3 purchase allowances + $2 purchase discounts.

Once you know net purchases, you can compute cost of goods available for sale.

To compute cost of goods available for sale:

$ 42	beginning inventory
+308	net purchases
$350	cost of goods available for sale

PROBLEM 6: In 20X2, MiCo purchased 30 units and returned 1 unit. What is MiCo's total units available for sale in 20X2?

SOLUTION 6: To find MiCo's total units available for sale, you must first compute its net units purchased:

To compute net purchases:

30	gross units purchased
− 1	unit returned
29	net units purchased

6	units in beginning inventory (same as MiCo's 20X1 ending inventory)
+29	net units purchased
35	units available for sale

PROBLEM 7: On December 31, 20X2, MiCo's physical count of inventory shows 7 units on hand. What is MiCo's 20X2 ending inventory? What is its 20X2 COGS?

SOLUTION 7: To find MiCo's 20X2 ending inventory, compute its weighted-average cost per unit:

$$\frac{\$350 * \text{ cost of goods available for sale}}{35 ** \text{ total units available for sale}} = \$10 \text{ weighted - avg cost per unit}$$

  * Computed in Solution 5.
** Computed in Solution 6.

To compute MiCo's 20X2 ending inventory:

7 units on hand at year end x $10 weighted-average cost per unit = $70 ending inventory

To compute MiCo's 20X2 cost of goods sold:

$ 42	beginning inventory
+308	net purchases
$350	cost of goods available for sale
− 70	ending inventory
$280	cost of goods sold

Alternative way to compute COGS:

35 units available for sale − 7 units on hand at year end =
28 units sold x $10 cost per unit = $280 cost of goods sold

Additional Illustrations of Ending Inventory and COGS Computations

Problems 8–11 illustrate weighted average costing for BuCo.

PROBLEM 8: BuCo's 20X4 beginning inventory is 100 units at $600. Gross purchases include 1,000 units at $13 per unit, 500 units at $10 per unit and 500 units at $7 per unit. There is no freight-in and no purchase discounts or allowances. BuCo returns 200 of the $13 units and 120 of the $10 units. What is BuCo's 20X4 cost of goods available for sale?

SOLUTION 8: To find BuCo's cost of goods available for sale, you must first compute its net purchases:

To Compute BuCo's 20X4 net purchases:

$21,500*	gross purchases
− 3,800**	purchase returns
$17,700	net purchases

```
*   1,000 units purchased x $13 unit cost =  $13,000
      500 units purchased x $10 unit cost =    5,000
  +   500 units purchased x $7 unit cost =  +  3,500
      2,000 gross units purchased             $21,500 gross purchases
```

```
**  200 units returned x $13 unit cost =    $2,600 purchase returns
   +120 units returned x $10 unit cost =    +1,200 purchase returns
    320 units returned                      $3,800 total purchase returns
```

To compute BuCo's 20X4 cost of goods available for sale:

$ 600	beginning inventory
+17,700	net purchases
$18,300	cost of goods available for sale

PROBLEM 9: On December 31, BuCo does a physical count of its stock and finds 900 units in ending inventory. Based on BuCo's ending inventory and the data in Problem 8, how many units did BuCo sell in 20X4?

SOLUTION 9: *To compute BuCo's units sold in 20X4:*

100	beginning inventory
2,000	gross purchases
– 320	returns
1,780	units available for sale
– 900	ending inventory
880	units sold in 20X4

PROBLEM 10: Using the computations from Problems 8 and 9, calculate BuCo's 20X4 cost per unit under weighted-average costing.

SOLUTION 10: *To compute:*

$$\frac{\$18,300 \text{ cost of goods available for sale}}{1,780^* \text{ units available for sale}} = \$10.28 \text{ weighted-average cost per unit in 20X4}$$

* 100 units in beginning inventory + 2,000 gross units purchased – 320 units returned = 1,780 units available for sale.

PROBLEM 11: Using the computations from Problems 9 and 10, calculate BuCo's 20X4 ending inventory and cost of goods sold.

SOLUTION 11: *To compute BuCo's 20X4 ending inventory:*

900 units on hand at year-end 20X4 x $10.28 per unit = $9,252 ending inventory for 20X4

To compute BuCo's 20X4 cost of goods sold:

$18,300	cost of goods available for sale
– 9,252	ending inventory
$ 9,048	cost of goods sold

Alternative way to compute BuCo's 20X4 cost of goods sold:

880 units sold in 20X4 x $10.28 per unit = $9,046* weighted-average cost of goods sold (rounded)

* The $2 difference from the other cost of goods sold computation is from rounding.

PROBLEM 12: CaCo begins operations in 20X6 and makes the following merchandise purchases in 20X6 and 20X7:

	20X6	**20X7**
March 1	400 @ $5	500 @ $8
July 1	900 @ $6	1,300 @ $11
	1,300	1,800

There are no purchase returns and no freight costs in either year. Year-end physical counts show 300 units in 20X6 ending inventory and 550 units in 20X7 ending inventory.

1. What will ending inventory be on CaCo's 20X6 balance sheet, and what will cost of goods sold be on CaCo's 20X6 income statement?

2. What will ending inventory be on CaCo's 20X7 balance sheet, and what will cost of goods sold be on CaCo's 20X7 income statement?

SOLUTION 12:

1. *To compute ending inventory for 20X6:*

$2,000	in March 1 purchase (400 units x $5 unit cost)
+5,400	in July 1 purchase (900 units x $6 unit cost)
$7,400	cost of goods available for sale

400	units purchased on March 1
+ 900	units purchased on July 1
1,300	units available for sale

$$\frac{\$7,400 \text{ cost of goods available for sale}}{1,300 \text{ units available for sale}} = \$5.69 \text{ (rounded) weighted-avg cost per unit in 20X6}$$

To compute 20X6 ending inventory:

300 units ending inventory, December 31, 20X6 x $5.69 cost per unit = $1,707 ending inventory for 20X6

To compute 20X6 cost of goods sold:

$7,400*	net purchases
−1,707	ending inventory
$5,693	cost of goods sold

* In a company's first year of operation, there is no beginning inventory; therefore net purchases are the same as cost of goods available for sale.

Alternative way to compute MiCo's 20X6 cost of goods sold:

1,300	net purchases (same as units available for sale in a company's first year of operation)
− 300	units in 20X6 ending inventory
1,000	units sold in 20X7

1,000 units sold x $5.69 per unit = $5,690* cost of goods sold

* the $3 difference from the other COGS computation is from rounding.

Ending inventory amount on CaCo's 20X6 balance sheet will be $1,707 (or $1,710 depending on rounding); cost of goods sold on CaCo's 20X6 income statement will be $5,693 (or $5,690 depending on rounding).

2. To compute for 20X7:

$ 1,707*	beginning inventory
+18,300**	net purchases
$20,007	cost of goods available for sale

* Same as 20X6 ending inventory, computed above.

** 500 units purchased on March 1, 20X7 x $8 unit cost =	$ 4,000
1,300 units purchased in July 1 x $11 unit cost =	+14,300
Net purchases	$18,300

$\dfrac{\$20,007 \text{ cost of goods available for sale}}{2,100* \text{ units available for sale}}$ = $9.53 (rounded) weighted-avg cost per unit

* 300	units in 20X7 beginning inventory
+1,800	net purchases (500 on March 1 + 1,300 on July 1)
2,100	units available for sale

To compute CaCo's 20X7 ending inventory:

550 units on hand, December 31, 20X7 x $9.53 per unit = $5,242 ending inventory in 20X7

$ 1,707	beginning inventory
+18,300	net purchases
$20,007	available for sale
− 5,242	ending inventory
$14,765	cost of goods sold

Alternative way to compute CaCo's 20X7 cost of goods sold:

300	units in 20X7 beginning inventory
+1,800	net purchases (500 on March 1 + 1,300 on July 1)
2,100	units available for sale
− 550	units in 20X7 ending inventory
1,550	units sold in 20X7

1,550 units sold x $9.53 per unit = $14,772* cost of goods sold

* The $7 difference from the other COGS computation is from rounding the unit cost of $9.53.

Ending inventory on CaCo's 20X7 balance sheet will be $5,242. COGS on CaCo's 20X6 income statement will be $14,765 because the total for cost of goods sold and ending inventory must equal the total cost of goods available for sale ($14,765 + $5,242 = $20,007).

How to Use Moving-Average Costing Under the Perpetual Method

Companies that use the perpetual method also use a weighted-average to find the cost per unit. However, the perpetual method requires cost of goods sold to be recorded each time there is a sale (unlike the periodic method where COGS is calculated only at year end). Thus, each time the company makes a purchase, it results in a new unit cost for the next sale—which is why it is called *moving-average* costing.

Average cost per unit under the perpetual method is computed the same way it is under the periodic method, but it is recomputed after each purchase instead of at year end.

$$\frac{\text{Cost of goods available for sale}}{\text{Units available for sale}} = \text{average cost per unit}$$

Average unit cost x number of units sold = cost of goods sold

PROBLEM 13: FeCo begins operations in 20X1 and decides to use the perpetual method. During 20X1, it makes the following merchandise purchases and sales:

January 3	Purchase of 800 units @ $12	= $ 9,600
February 17	Purchase of 1,200 units @ $15	= $18,000
March 10	Sale of 600 units @ $20	= $12,000
April 7	Purchase of 1,000 units @ $17	= $17,000
May 19	Sale of 1,100 units @ $22	= $24,200

What is FeCo's cost of goods sold (a) for the sale on March 10 and (b) for the sale on May 19?

SOLUTION 13: *Moving-average* costing is easiest to illustrate by looking at the Inventory account. The computations beneath show how the amounts in the account were derived. Note that when you use moving-average costing, the average unit cost under "Balance" changes or *moves* after each purchase. Small differences between the Inventory account amounts and computed amounts are due to rounding.

a. Cost of goods sold for the March 10 sale will appear in the Inventory account as follows (computations are shown below):

Inventory Account								
	Purchases			**Sales**			**Balance**		
Date	**Units**	**Unit Cost**	**Total Cost**	**Units**	**Unit Cost**	**Total Cost**	**Units**	**Unit Cost**	**Total Cost**
January 3	800	12.00	9,600.00				800	12.00	9,600.00
February 17	1,200	15.00	18,000.00				2,000	13.80	27,600.00
March 10				600	13.80*	8,280.00	1,400	13.80	19,320.00

* This is the COGS per unit.

First compute the cost of goods available for the March 10 sale:

$ 9,600	January 3 purchase
+18,000	February 17 purchases
$27,600	cost of goods available for sale on March 10

Then compute the number of units available for the March 10 sale:

800	January 3 purchase
+1,200	February 17 purchase
2,000	units available for sale on March 10

Finally, use the computed amounts to find cost per unit and cost of goods sold for the March 10 sale.

$$\frac{\$27,600 \text{ cost of goods available for sale}}{2,000 \text{ units available for sale}} = \$13.80 \text{ cost per unit}$$

600 units sold x $13.80 unit cost = **$8,280 COGS for the March 10 sale**

b. Cost of goods sold for the May 19 sale will appear in the Inventory account as follows (computations are shown below):

Inventory Account									
	Purchases			Sales			Balance		
Date	Units	Unit Cost	Total Cost	Units	Unit Cost	Total Cost	Units	Unit Cost	Total Cost
January 3	800	12.00	9,600.00				800	12.00	9,600.00
February 17	1,200	15.00	18,000.00				2,000	13.80	27,600.00
March 10				600	13.80	8,280.00	1,400	13.80	19,320.00
April 7	1,000	17.00	17,000.00				2,400	15.13	36,320.00[1]
May 19				1,100	15.13*	16,643.00	1,300	15.13	19,677.00[2]

* This is the COGS per unit

[1] $19,320 + $17,000 = $36,320
[2] $36,320 − $16,643 = $19,677

First compute the cost of goods available for the May 19 sale:

$19,320   cost of goods available for sale (balance)
+17,000   April 7 purchases
$36,320   cost of goods available for sale on May 19

Then compute the number of units available for the May 19 sale:

1,400   units available for sale (balance)
+1,000   units purchased on April 7
2,400   units available for sale on May 19

Finally, use the computed amounts to find cost per unit and cost of goods sold for the May 19 sale.

$$\frac{\$36,320 \text{ cost of goods available for sale}}{2,400 \text{ units available for sale}} = \$15.13 \text{ cost per unit}$$

1,100 units sold x $15.13 unit cost = **$16,643 COGS for the May 19 sale**

PROBLEM 14: HeCo begins operations in July and uses the moving average method. It purchases 300 units of merchandise at $5 per unit on August 12 and 2,000 units at $9 per unit on November 4. HeCo sells 200 units at $8 per unit on September 16 and 1,200 units at $13 per unit on December 17. All purchases and sales are cash transactions. What journal entries does HeCo record, and on what dates does HeCo record them?

SOLUTION 14: Here again the Inventory account is used to illustrate *moving average* costing. The computations beneath show how the amounts in the account were derived. Note that when you use *moving average,* the average unit cost under "Balance" changes or *moves* with each purchase. Small differences between the Inventory account amounts and computed amounts are due to rounding.

Here is how the inventory account will appear on August 12:

Inventory Account								
	Purchases			**Sales**			**Balance**		
Date	**Units**	**Unit Cost**	**Total Cost**	**Units**	**Unit Cost**	**Total Cost**	**Units**	**Unit Cost**	**Total Cost**
August 12	300	5.00	1,500.00				300	5.00	1,500.00

To record the August 12 purchase
Inventory   1,500
    Cash   1,500
(300 units x $5 unit cost)

Here is how the inventory account will appear on September 16:

Inventory Account								
	Purchases			**Sales**			**Balance**		
Date	**Units**	**Unit Cost**	**Total Cost**	**Units**	**Unit Cost**	**Total Cost**	**Units**	**Unit Cost**	**Total Cost**
August 12	300	5.00	1,500.00				300	5.00	1,500.00
September 16				200	5.00*	1,000.00	100	5.00	500.00[1]

       * COGS per unit   [1] $1,500 – $1,000 = $500

To record the September 16 sale
Cash   1,600
    Sales Revenue   1,600
(200 units x $8 unit sales price)

Cost of Goods Sold   1,000
    Inventory   1,000
(200 units x $5 unit cost)

Here is how the Inventory account will appear on November 4:

	Purchases			Sales			Balance		
Date	Units	Unit Cost	Total Cost	Units	Unit Cost	Total Cost	Units	Unit Cost	Total Cost
August 12	300	5.00	1,500.00				300	5.00	1,500.00
September 16				200	5.00	1,000.00	100	5.00	500.00
November 4	2,000	9.00	18,000.00				2,100	8.81	18,500.00

Inventory Account

To record the November 4 purchase

Inventory	18,000	
Cash		18,000

(2,000 units x $9 unit cost)

Here is how the Inventory account will appear on December 17:

Inventory Account

	Purchases			Sales			Balance		
Date	Units	Unit Cost	Total Cost	Units	Unit Cost	Total Cost	Units	Unit Cost	Total Cost
August 12	300	5.00	1,500.00				300	5.00	1,500.00
September 16				200	5.00	1,000.00	100	5.00	500.00
November 4	2,000	9.00	18,000.00				2,100	8.81	18,500.00
December 17				1,200	8.81*	10,572.00	900	8.81	7,928.00[1]

* COGS per unit   [1] $18,500 – $10,572 = $7,928

Computations for cost of goods sold for the December 17 sale:

100 units available for sale on September 16 (300 units purchasd on August 12 – 200 units sold on September 16) x $5 unit cost = $500 cost of goods available for sale on September 16

$ 500	cost of goods available for sale on September 16
+18,000	November 4 purchase
$18,500	cost of goods available for sale on December 17

100	units available for sale in September 16
+ 2,000	units purchased on November 4
2,100	units available for sale on December 17

$$\frac{\$18,500 \text{ cost of goods available for sale}}{2,100 \text{ units available for sale}} = \$8.81 \text{ cost per unit (rounded)}$$

1,200 units sold in December x $8.81 unit cost = $10,572 December COGS

To record the December 17 sale

Cash	15,600	
Sales Revenue		15,600
(1,200 units x $13 unit sales price)		

Cost of Goods Sold	10,572	
Inventory		10,572
(1,200 units x $8.81 unit cost)		

Summary

- *To find ending inventory and cost of goods sold under the periodic method:* Compute both amounts at year end using weighted-average costing, as follows:

  1. Compute total cost of goods available for sale.

  2. Compute total units available for sale.

  3. Compute the *weighted-average* cost per unit (total cost of goods available for sale divided by total units available for sale).

  4. To compute ending inventory, multiply the number of units in ending inventory (shown in the physical count) by the weighted-average cost per unit.

  5. To compute cost of goods sold, subtract ending inventory from cost of goods available for sale.

- *To find ending inventory and cost of goods sold under the perpetual method:* Simply use the balances of in the Inventory and Cost of Goods Sold accounts respectively.

QUIZ 1 INVENTORY COSTING: THE WEIGHTED-AVERAGE AND MOVING-AVERAGE METHODS

Problem I.

On January 12, 20X0, KuCo begins operations and purchases 700 units of merchandise at $4 each. On February 6, it purchases 1,200 units at $5 each, and on March 14, it sells 1,100 units at $15 each. What is KuCo's cost for the March 14 sale under the perpetual method? Fill in the blank Inventory account with each amount given and each amount that you compute.

Inventory Account									
	Purchases			Sales			Balance		
Date	Units	Unit Cost	Total Cost	Units	Unit Cost	Total Cost	Units	Unit Cost	Total Cost

Problem II.

ToCo begins business in October, 20X9. On October 23, it buys 800 units of merchandise at $12 a unit; on November 4, it sells 500 units for $9,500; on November 21, it purchases 2,000 units at $14 per unit; and on December 6, it sells 900 units for $19,000. If ToCo uses the periodic method, what amount will appear on ToCo's 20X9 income statement for cost of goods sold?

Problem III.

ZiCo begins operations in September 20X4 and makes the cash purchases and sales listed below. Prepare ZiCo's journal entries assuming that it uses the perpetual method. Fill in the blank Inventory account and show any computations needed to arrive at the amounts.

	Purchases	**Sales**
20X4		
October 23	600 @ $3	
November 5	900 @ $4	
December 11		700 @ $7
20X5		
January 10	1,800 @ $6	
February 2		1,100 @ $10

Inventory Account									
	Purchases			**Sales**			**Balance**		
Date	**Units**	**Unit Cost**	**Total Cost**	**Units**	**Unit Cost**	**Total Cost**	**Units**	**Unit Cost**	**Total Cost**

Problem IV.

SuCo starts 20X4 with 5,000 units of merchandise in beginning inventory at $13 per unit cost. Purchases and sales during 20X4 are as follows:

	Purchases	**Sales**
• February 14	1,500 @ $16	
• May 22		2,200 @ $30
• September 2	1,000 @ $17	
• November 15	1,200 @ $18	
• December 9		3,300 @ $40

If SuCo uses the perpetual method, how much will ending inventory be on its December 31, 20X4 balance sheet? How much will cost of goods sold be on its 20X4 income statement? Fill in the blank Inventory account with each amount given and each amount that you compute.

Inventory Account									
	Purchases			**Sales**			**Balance**		
Date	**Units**	**Unit Cost**	**Total Cost**	**Units**	**Unit Cost**	**Total Cost**	**Units**	**Unit Cost**	**Total Cost**

Problem V.

ViCo gives you the following data:

• December 31, 20X3	Ending inventory of 400 units	$ 6,800
• January, 4, 20X4	Purchase of 500 units @ $19	9,500
• January 4, 20X4	Freight for purchase	300
• June 23, 20X4	Sale of 300 units @ $30	9,000
• December 24, 20X4	Purchase of 700 units @ $20	14,000
• December 27, 20X4	Return of 100 units @ $20	2,000

On December 31, 20X4 ViCo has 1,200 units on hand. How much is cost of goods sold on its 20X4 income statement under the periodic method?

QUIZ 1 Solutions and Explanations

Problem I.

KuCo computes its 20X0 cost of goods sold under the perpetual method with *moving-average* costing. Under the perpetual method, KuCo must record the cost of goods sold each time it makes a sale. This cost will change each time KuCo purchases merchandise. Therefore, after each purchase, KuCo must recompute the average unit cost on which COGS is based. This constant recomputing results in a *moving average* unit cost.

	Inventory Account								
	Purchases			Sales			Balance		
Date	Units	Unit Cost	Total Cost	Units	Unit Cost	Total Cost	Units	Unit Cost	Total Cost
January 12	700	4.00	2,800.00				700	4.00	2,800.00
February 6	1,200	5.00	6,000.00				1,900	4.63	8,800.00
March 14				1,100	4.63	5,093.00	800	463	3,707.00*

* $8,800 – $5.093 = $3,707

To compute cost per unit for the March 14 sale:

$2,800	January purchase (700 units x $4)
+6,000	February purchase (1,200 units x $5)
$8,800	cost of goods available for sale

700	units purchased in January
+1,200	units purchased in February
1,900	units available for sale

$$\frac{\$8,800 \text{ cost of goods available for sale}}{1,900 \text{ units available for sale}} = \$4.63 \text{ cost per unit}$$

To compute cost of goods sold for the March 14 sale:

1,100 units sold x $4.63 unit cost = **$5,093 COGS**

Problem II.

Under the periodic method, ToCo's 20X9 cost of goods sold is computed using *weighted average* costing. At year end, ToCo computes the average cost per unit for the year, then uses this cost to compute cost of goods sold, as follows:

$ 9,600	October 23 purchase (800 units x $12 unit cost)
+28,000	November 21 purchase (2,000 units x $14 unit cost)
37,600	cost of goods available for sale

800	units purchased on October 23
+ 2,000	units purchased on November 21
$ 2,800	units available for sale

$$\frac{\$37,600 \text{ cost of goods available for sale}}{2,800 \text{ units available for sale}} = \$13.43 \text{ cost per unit for 20X9}$$

1,400 units sold (500 units in November + 900 units in December) x $13.43 cost per unit = **$18,802 COGS**

On ToCo's 20X9 income statement, COGS will be $18,802.

Problem III.

Because ZiCo uses the perpetual method, it must record the cost of goods sold each time it makes a sale. This cost will change every time ZiCo purchases merchandise. Therefore, after each purchase, ZiCo recomputes the average unit cost on which COGS is based. This constant recomputing results in a *moving-average* unit cost. Small differences between the Inventory account amounts and computed amounts are due to rounding.

Inventory Account									
	Purchases			**Sales**			**Balance**		
Date	Units	Unit Cost	Total Cost	Units	Unit Cost	Total Cost	Units	Unit Cost	Total Cost
20X4									
October 23	600	3.00	1,800.00				600	3.00	1,800.00
November 5	900	4.00	3,600.00				1,500	3.60	5,400.00
December 11				700	3.60	2,520.00	800	3.60	2,880.00[1]
December 31 Ending Inventory									2,880.00
Cost of goods sold						2,520.00			
20X5									
January 1 (Beginning Inventory)							800	3.60	2,880.00
January 10	1,800	6.00	10,800.00				2,600	5.26	13,680.00
February 2				1,100	5.26	5,786.00	1,500	5.26	7,894.00[2]

[1] $5,400 – $2,520 = $2,880
[2] 13,680 – $5,786 = $7,894

For 20X4

To record the October 23 purchase

Inventory	1,800	
Cash		1,800

(600 units x $3 unit cost)

To record the November 5 purchase

Inventory	3,600	
Cash		3,600

(900 units x $4 unit cost)

To compute weighted-average cost per unit for the December 11 sale:

$1,800	October purchases
+3,600	November purchases
$5,400	cost of goods available for sale

600	units purchased in October
+ 900	units purchased in November
1,500	total units available for sale

$$\frac{\$5,400 \text{ cost of goods available for sale}}{1,500 \text{ units available for sale}} = \$3.60 \text{ weighted-avg cost per unit}$$

To compute COGS for the December 11 sale:

700 units sold x $3.60 unit cost = **$2,520 COGS**

To record the December 11 sale
Cash	4,900	
Sales Revenue		4,900

(700 units sold x $7 unit sales price)

Cost of Goods Sold	2,520	
Inventory		2,520

(700 units x $3.60 unit cost)

For 20X5
To record the January 10 purchase
Inventory	10,800	
Cash		10,800

(1,800 units x $6 unit cost)

To compute cost per unit for the February 2 sale:

800 units in 20X5 beginning inventory x $3.60 unit cost =
$2,880 goods available before January 10 purchase

$ 2,880	beginning inventory, January 1, 20X5
+10,800	January 10 purchase
$13,680	cost of goods available for sale on January 10

800	20X5 beginning inventory
+ 1,800	units purchased on January 10
2,600	units available for sale

$$\frac{\$13,680 \text{ cost of goods available for sale}}{2,600 \text{ units available for sale}} = \$5.26 \text{ (rounded) weighted-avg cost per unit}$$

To compute COGS for the February 2 sale:

1,100 units sold x $5.26 unit cost = $5,786 (rounded)

To record the February 2 sale
Cash   11,000
    Sales Revenue   11,000
(1,100 units sold x $10 sale price)

Cost of Goods Sold   5,786
    Inventory   5,786
(1,100 units x $5.26 unit cost)

Problem IV.

Because SuCo uses the perpetual method, it must record the cost of goods sold each time it makes a sale. This cost will change every time SuCo purchases merchandise. Therefore, after each purchase, SuCo recomputes the average unit cost on which COGS is based. This constant recomputing results in a moving average unit cost. Small differences between the Inventory account amounts and computed amounts are due to rounding.

Inventory Account									
	Purchases			Sales			Balance		
Date	Units	Unit Cost	Total Cost	Units	Unit Cost	Total Cost	Units	Unit Cost	Total Cost
January 1 Beginning Inventory							5,000	13.00	65,000.00
February 14	1,500	16.00	24,000.00				6,500	13.69	89,000.00
May 22				2,200	13.69	30,118.00	4,300	13.69	58,882.00[1]
September 2	1,000	17.00	17,000.00				5,300	14.32	75,882.00
November 15	1,200	18.00	21,600.00				6,500	15.00	97,482.00
December 9				3,300	15.00	49,500.00	3,200	15.00	47,982.00[2]
December 31 Ending Inventory									47,982.00
Cost of goods sold						79,618.00			

[1] $89,000 − $30,118 = $58,882
[2] $97,482 − $49,500 = $47,982

Cost of goods sold computations for the May 22 sale:

$65,000   20X4 beginning inventory (same as 20X3
            ending inventory)
+24,000   February 14 purchase (1,500 units x $16 unit cost)
$89,000   cost of goods available for sale

5,000   units 20X4 beginning inventory
+1,500   units purchased on February 14
6,500   units available for sale

$$\frac{\$89,000 \text{ cost of goods available for sale}}{6,500 \text{ units available for sale}} = \$13.69 \text{ cost per unit}$$

2,200 units sold x $13.69 unit cost = **$30,118 COGS**

Computation of unit cost after September 2 purchase:

$$\frac{\$75,882 \text{ cost of goods available for sale}}{5,300 \text{ units available for sale}} = \$14.32 \text{ cost per unit}$$

Cost of goods sold computations for the December 9 sale:

$89,000   Cost of goods available for sale before May 22 sale
−30,118   Cost of goods sold on May 22
$58,882   Cost of goods available for sale after May 22

$58,882   cost of goods available for sale after May 22
17,000   September 2 purchase (1,000 units x $17 unit cost)
+21,600   November 15 purchase (1,200 units x $18 unit cost)
$97,482   cost of goods available for sale

4,300   units available for sale after May 22
1,000   units purchased on September 2
+ 1,200   units purchased on November 15
6,500   units available for December 9 sale

$$\frac{\$97,482 \text{ cost of goods available for sale}}{6,500 \text{ units available for sale}} = \$15.00 \text{ cost per unit (rounded)}$$

continued

3,300 units x $15 unit cost = **$49,500 COGS**

To find ending inventory for 20X4, simply use the balance in the account on December 31:

Ending inventory for 20X4 is $47,982 (rounded).

To verify COGS for 20X4:

$30,118	cost of goods sold for May 22 sale
+49,500	cost of goods sold for December 9 sale
$79,618	cost of goods sold for 20X4

Problem V.

Under the periodic method, ViCo's 20X4 cost of goods sold is computed using *weighted average*. At year end, ViCo computes ending inventory and cost of goods sold.

To compute net purchases:

$23,500*	gross purchases
– 2,000	purchase returns
21,500	subtotal
+ 300	freight-in
$21,800	net purchases

* $9,500 January 4 purchase + $14,000 December 24 purchase.

To compute cost of goods available for sale:

$ 6,800	beginning inventory (January 1, 20X4, same as 20X3 ending inventory)
+21,800	net purchases
$28,600	cost of goods available for sale

```
   400     units beginning inventory (January 1, 20X4,
           same as 20X3 ending inventory)
 +1,200    units purchased during 20X4
  1,600    units
 -  100    units returned
  1,500    units available for sale
```

$$\frac{\$28,600 \text{ cost of goods available for sale}}{1,500 \text{ units available for sale}} = \$19.07 \text{ (rounded) cost per unit}$$

1,200 units x $ 19.07 unit cost = $22,884 ending inventory

300 units sold x $ 19.07 unit cost = $5,721 COGS

QUIZ 2   INVENTORY COSTING: THE WEIGHTED-AVERAGE AND MOVING-AVERAGE METHODS

Problem I.

YoCo starts business in September, 20X7. On October 2, it buys 1,000 units of merchandise at $14 a unit, and on November 14, it sells 900 units for $24,200. On December 1, it purchases 1,800 units at $19 a unit, and on December 16, YoCo sells 400 units for $19,000. If YoCo uses the perpetual method, what is ending inventory on its December 31, 20X7 balance sheet? Fill in the blank Inventory account with each amount given and each amount that you compute.

Inventory Account									
	Purchases			Sales			Balance		
Date	Units	Unit Cost	Total Cost	Units	Unit Cost	Total Cost	Units	Unit Cost	Total Cost

Problem II.

WeCo begins business in August, 20X2. On September 18, it buys 1,500 units of merchandise at $10 a unit. On October 6, WeCo sells 900 units for $12,000, and on November 1, WeCo purchases 2,500 units at $13 a unit. On December 26, WeCo sells 1,900 units for $29,000. If WeCo uses the perpetual method, what is the cost of goods sold on its 20X2 income statement? Fill in the blank Inventory account with each amount given and each amount that you compute.

Inventory Account									
	Purchases			Sales			Balance		
Date	Units	Unit Cost	Total Cost	Units	Unit Cost	Total Cost	Units	Unit Cost	Total Cost

Problem III.

LuCo begins operations in October, 20X2 and uses the periodic method. Using the data below, compute ending inventory for LuCo's December 31, 20X2 and December 31, 20X3 balance sheets.

20X2	Quantity	Unit cost
November 20 purchase	1,300	$4
December 18 purchase	4,400	5

In 20X2 LuCo sold 3,700 units. A physical count of its inventory on December 31 showed 2,000 units on hand.

20X3	Quantity	Unit cost
March 4 purchase	2,200	$ 6
August 13 purchase	4,400	7
November 10 purchase	7,900	10

In 20X3 LuCo sold 12,000 units. A physical count of its inventory on December 31 showed 4,500 units.

Problem IV.

KaCo, which uses the periodic method, begins operations in November 20X7 and shows the following data:

- Nov. 27: 1,500 units purchased for $11,500 plus $500 for shipping, all cash
- Dec. 3: 600 units sold for $8,400 on account
- Dec. 5: $700 cash allowance received for defects in Nov. 27 purchase
- Dec. 11: 2,000 units purchased on account @ $11, F.O.B. destination
- Dec. 19: 1,800 units sold for $27,000 cash
- Dec. 22: 100 units returned from Dec. 11 purchase
- Dec. 29: payment made for Dec. 11 purchase
- Dec. 30: accounts receivable from Dec. 3 sale collected
- Dec. 31: physical count of inventory showed 1,000 units on hand

1. Prepare the journal entries for the merchandise transactions below.

2. Prepare the journal entry to close out KaCo's inventory-related accounts to Cost of Goods Sold and to adjust KaCo's Inventory account so that the balance is ending inventory.

Problem V.

BiCo's 20X8 beginning inventory is 3,000 units that have an average cost of $17 each. On January 19, 20X8, BiCo sells 1,200 units for cash at $25 each. On January 25, it purchases 4,000 units on account at $19 per unit, and on January 30, it sells 2,500 units for $75,000 on account. BiCo uses the perpetual method. Prepare BiCo's journal entries for the three January transactions. Fill in the blank Inventory account with each amount given and each amount that you compute.

Inventory Account									
	Purchases			Sales			Balance		
Date	Units	Unit Cost	Total Cost	Units	Unit Cost	Total Cost	Units	Unit Cost	Total Cost

QUIZ 2   *Solutions and Explanations*

Problem I.

Because YoCo uses the perpetual method, it must record the cost of goods sold each time it makes a sale. This cost will change each time YoCo purchases merchandise. Therefore, after each purchase, YoCo recomputes the average unit cost on which COGS is based. This constant recomputing results in a *moving average* unit cost. Small differences between the Inventory account amounts and computed amounts are due to rounding.

Inventory Account								
	Purchases			**Sales**			**Balance**		
Date	**Units**	**Unit Cost**	**Total Cost**	**Units**	**Unit Cost**	**Total Cost**	**Units**	**Unit Cost**	**Total Cost**
October 2	1,000	14.00	14,000.00				1,000	14.00	14,000.00
November 14				900	14.00	12,600.00	100	14.00	1,400.00
December 1	1,800	19.00	34,200.00				1,900	18.74	35,600.00
December 16				400	18.74	7,496.00	1,500	18.74	28,104.00
December 31 Ending inventory									28,104.00

Computations for ending inventory:

$ 1,400   cost of goods available after the November 14 sale
+34,200   December 1 purchase
$35,600   cost of goods available before the December 16 sale

 100   units available for sale after the November 14 sale
+ 1,800   units purchased on December 16
 1,900   units available before the December 16 sale

$$\frac{\$35,600 \text{ cost of goods available for sale}}{1,900 \text{ units available for sale}} = 18.74 \text{ cost per unit}$$

400 units x $18.74 unit cost = **$7,496 COGS**

$35,600   cost of goods available for sale
– 7,496   cost of goods sold for the December 15 sale (rounded)
$28,104   cost of goods available for sale after December 15

Because YoCo makes no further purchases or sales during 20X7, the balance remaining after the December 16 sale—1,500 units costing $28,104—becomes ending inventory on December 31.

Problem II.

Because WeCo uses the perpetual method, it must record the cost of goods sold each time it makes a sale. This cost will change each time WeCo purchases merchandise. Therefore, after each purchase, WeCo recomputes the average unit cost on which COGS is based. This constant recomputing results in a *moving-average* unit cost. Small differences between the Inventory account amounts and computed amounts are due to rounding.

Inventory Account										
	Purchases			**Sales**			**Balance**			
Date	**Units**	**Unit Cost**	**Total Cost**	**Units**	**Unit Cost**	**Total Cost**	**Units**	**Unit Cost**	**Total Cost**	
September 18	1,500	10.00	15,000.00				1,500	10.00	15,000.00	
October 6				900	10.00	9,000.00	600	10.00	6,000.00	
November 1	2,500	13.00	32,500.00				3,100	12.42	38,500.00	
December 26				1,900	12.42	23,598.00	1,200	12.42	14,902.00	
December 31 Ending Inventory									14,902.00	
Cost of goods sold						32,598.00				

Computations for cost of goods sold:

$15,000   September 18 purchase (1,500 units x $10 unit cost)
– 9,000   October 6 sale (900 units x $10 unit cost)
$ 6,000   cost of goods available for sale after October 6 (balance)
+32,500   November 1 purchase (2,500 units x $13 unit cost)
$38,500   cost of goods available for sale after November 1 (balance)

1,500 units available for sale on September 18
− 900 units sold on October 6
600 units available for sale
+2,500 units purchased on November 1
3,100 units available for sale after November 1

$$\frac{38,500 \text{ goods available for sale}}{3,100 \text{ units available for sale}} = \$12.42 \text{ cost per unit}$$

1,900 units x $12.42 unit cost = $23,598 (rounded) cost of goods sold

$ 9,000 cost of goods sold for October 6 sale
+23,598 COGS for December 26 sale (rounded)
$32,598 COGS on WeCo's 20X2 income statement (rounded)

Problem III.

Under the periodic method, LuCo's 20X0 ending inventory is computed using *weighted average costing*. At year end, LuCo computes the average cost per unit for the year, then multiplies this cost by the number of items found in the physical count of inventory on December 31. The result is ending inventory.

For 20X2
December 31, 20X2
$ 5,200 November 20 purchase (1,300 units x $4 unit cost)
+22,000 December 18 purchase (4,400 units x $5 unit cost)
$27,200 cost of goods available for sale in 20X2

1,300 units purchased on November 20
+ 4,400 units purchased on December 18
5,700 units available for sale in 20X2

$$\frac{27,200 \text{ cost of goods available for sale}}{5,700 \text{ units available for sale}} = \$4.77 \text{ weighted-average cost per unit}$$

2,000* units x $4.77 unit cost = **$9,540 ending inventory in 20X2**

* From the year-end physical count given in the problem.

For 20X3

$ 13,200 March 4 purchase (2,200 units x $6 unit cost)

    30,800 August 13 purchase (4,400 units x $7 unit cost)

+ 79,000 November 10 purchase (7,900 units x $10 unit cost)

$123,000 net purchases in 20X3

$ 9,540 beginning inventory, January 1, 20X3 (same as ending inventory, December 31, 20X2)

+123,000 net purchases in 20X3

$132,540 cost of goods available for sale

   2,000 units in 20X3 beginning inventory (same as 20X2 ending inventory)

   2,200 units purchased on March 4

   4,400 units purchased on August 13

+ 7,900 units purchased on November 10

  16,500 units available for sale in 20X3

$$\frac{\$132,540 \text{ cost of goods available for sale}}{16,500 \text{ units available for sale}} = \$8.03 \text{ cost per unit cost}$$

4,500* units x $8.03 unit cost = **$36,135 ending inventory for 20X3**

* From the year-end physical count given in the problem.

Problem IV.

Under the periodic method, KaCo's 20X0 ending inventory is computed using *weighted average* costing. At year end, KaCo computes the average cost per unit for the year, then uses this cost to compute ending inventory.

1. The journal entries for KaCo's merchandise transactions are:

To record the November 27 purchase

Purchases	11,500	
Freight-In	500	
Cash		12,000

To record the December 3 purchase

Accounts Receivable	8,400	
Sales Revenue		8,400

To record the December 5 purchase allowance

Cash	700	
Purchase Allowances		700

To record the December 11 purchase

Purchases	22,000	
Accounts Payable		22,000

(2,000 units purchased x $11 unit cost)

To record the December 19 sale

Cash	27,000	
Sales Revenue		27,000

To record the December 22 return

Accounts Payable	1,100	
Purchase Returns		1,100

(100 units returned x $11 unit cost)

To record the December 29 payment of the December 11 purchase

Accounts Payable	20,900	
Cash		20,900

($22,000 purchase of Dec. 11 – $1,100 return of Dec. 22)

To record the December 30 receipt of payment for the December 3 sale

Cash	8,400	
Accounts Receivable		8,400

2. The journal entry to close out KaCo's inventory-related accounts to Cost of Goods Sold and to adjust the Inventory account so that the balance is ending inventory is:

Ending Inventory	9,470[1]	
Purchase Returns	1,100	
Purchase Allowances	700	
Cost of Goods Sold	**22,730**[2] (rounded)	
Purchases		33,500*
Freight-In		500

(Note that there is no credit to Beginning Inventory because it is KaCo's first year of operation and there is none.)

* $11,500	purchase on November 27	
+22,000	purchase on December 11	
$33,500	total purchases	

[1]*Computations for ending inventory:*

$33,500	purchases
– 1,800	purchase returns and allowances (1,100 + 700)
$31,700	subtotal
+ 500	freight-in
$32,200	net purchases (same as cost of goods available for sale in a company's first year of operation)

Units available for sale:

1,500	units purchased on November 27
+ 2,000	units purchased on December 11
3,500	subtotal
– 100	units returned on December 22
3,400	total units available for sale in 20X7

continued

$$\frac{\$32,200 \text{ cost of goods available for sale in 20X7}}{3,400 \text{ units available for sale}} = \$9.47 \text{ weighted-average cost per unit}$$

1,000 units on hand at year end x $9.47 unit cost = $9,470 ending inventory for 20X7

[2] *Computations for cost of goods sold:*

$32,200	cost of goods available for sale
− 9,470	ending inventory
$22,730	cost of goods sold

Problem V.

Because BiCo uses the perpetual method, it must record the cost of goods sold each time it makes a sale. This cost will change each time BiCo purchases merchandise. Therefore, after each purchase, BiCo recomputes the average unit cost on which COGS is based. This constant recomputing results in a *moving average* unit cost. Small differences between the Inventory account amounts and computed amounts are due to rounding.

	Purchases			Sales			Balance		
Date	Units	Unit Cost	Total Cost	Units	Unit Cost	Total Cost	Units	Unit Cost	Total Cost
January 1 (Beginning Inventory)							3,000	17.00	51,000.00
January 19				1,200	17.00	20,400.00	1,800	17.00	30,600.00
January 25	4,000	19.00	76,000.00				5,800	18.38	106,600.00
January 30				2,500	18.38	45,950.00	3,300	18.38	60,650.00

Inventory Account

<u>To record the January 19 sale</u>

Cash	30,000	
Sales Revenue		30,000

(1,200 units x $25 sales price)

Cost of Goods Sold	20,400	
Inventory		20,400

(1,200 units x $17 unit cost)

<u>To record the January 25 purchase</u>

Inventory	76,000	
Accounts Payable		76,000

(4,000 units purchased x $19 per unit)

Cost of goods sold computations for the January 30 sale:

$ 51,000	beginning inventory (January 1, 20X8)
– 20,400	cost of goods sold for January 19 sale
$ 30,600	available for sale
+ 76,000	January 25 purchase
$106,600	cost of goods available for January 30 sale

3,000	units in beginning inventory (January 1, 20X8)
– 1,200	units sold on January 19
1,800	subtotal
+ 4,000	units purchased on January 25
5,800	units available for January 30 sale

$$\frac{\$106,600 \text{ cost of goods available for sale}}{5,800 \text{ units available for sale}} = \$18.38 \text{ cost per unit}$$

2,500 units x $18.38 unit cost = **$45,950 COGS**

<u>To record the January 30 sale</u>

Accounts Receivable	75,000	
Sales Revenue		75,000

(2,500 units x $3 per unit)

Cost of Goods Sold	45,950	
Inventory		45,950

(2,500 units x $18.38 unit cost)

INVENTORY COSTING USING THE FIFO METHOD

Introduction

To compute cost of goods sold (COGS) for the income statement (under expenses) and the cost of ending inventory for the balance sheet (under assets), most companies may use one of three costing methods: average (weighted average for the periodic method or moving average for the perpetual method), first-in first-out (FIFO), or last-in first-out (LIFO).

This section covers FIFO costing under both the periodic and perpetual methods.

How to Use FIFO Costing

FIFO makes no attempt to match revenue from sales with the actual cost of the merchandise that was sold. Instead, it is based on the assumption that the first units that a company buys ("first in") are the first units that it sells ("first out").

To apply FIFO, a company must list the units available for sale and their unit cost *in the order in which they were purchased*.

For example, your company began operation in December, 20X0 and made the following purchases:

Purchase date	Units purchased	Unit cost
December 15	100	$3
December 17	70	4
December 19	150	5

On December 20, your company sells 110 units. To compute cost of goods sold using FIFO costing, cost out the units from the first purchase (100 units at $3 per unit), then the units from the second purchase (10 units at $4 per unit) and so on. To illustrate:

Total units sold in 20X1: 110

	Purchase date	Units sold	Unit cost	Total cost
From first purchase........December 15		100	$3	$300
From second purchase......December 17		+10	4	+ 40
Total		110	COGS	$340

Computing Ending Inventory under FIFO

To compute ending inventory under FIFO, start with the unit cost of the last purchase made, then the next-to-last purchase, etc., working backward. This is done because FIFO assumes that the first items purchased (first in) were the first ones sold (first out). As a result, ending inventory includes the items purchased most recently.

FIFO Costing Under the Periodic Method

Companies that use the periodic method base ending inventory on the physical count of merchandise at year end. The cost of ending inventory is used to compute cost of goods sold.

In a company's first year of operation, there is no beginning inventory, so COGS is based on purchases for the year less ending inventory.

Net purchases (the same as goods available for sale in Year 1)
– Ending inventory
Cost of goods sold

PROBLEM 1: DuCo began operation in 20X1. For inventory, it uses the periodic method and FIFO costing. During 20X1, DuCo purchases merchandise as follows:

Purchase date	Units purchased	Unit cost	Total cost
March 3............400		$5	$ 2,000
July 7 900		6	5,400
October 17..........+ 800		7	+ 5,600
Total 2,100			$13,000

The year-end physical count of merchandise shows 600 units in ending inventory. What is DuCo's 20X1 cost of goods sold?

SOLUTION 1: To determine COGS, DuCo must first find ending inventory, which the physical count showed as 600 units. Under FIFO, the cost of units in ending inventory begins with the cost of the units in the last purchase—October 17 in DuCo's case.

To compute ending inventory:

600 units from the last purchase (on October 17) x $7 per unit = $4,200 ending inventory

To compute cost of goods sold:

	Units	**Cost**
Net purchases*	2,100	$13,000
– Ending inventory	– 600	– 4,200
Cost of goods sold	1,500	$ 8,800

* In a company's first year of business, this is the same as cost of goods available for sale.

To prove cost of goods sold: FIFO costing assumes that the first units purchased were the first ones sold. Therefore, to prove cost of goods sold, start with the cost of units in beginning inventory, add the cost of units in the first purchase, then the second purchase, then the third purchase, etc., until the total number of units sold for the year is reached.

DuCo reached total units sold for the year with units from its third purchase.

Total units sold in 20X1: 1,500

	Purchase date	**Units sold**	**Unit cost**	**Total cost**
From first purchase. . . . . March 3		400	$5	$2,000
From second purchase. . . . . . July 7		900	6	5,400
From third purchase . . . . October 17		+ 200*	7	+1,400
Total		1,500	**COGS**	**$8,800**

*	800	units in original October 17 purchase
	–600	units remaining in ending inventory
	200	units from October 17 purchase sold in 20X1

After a company's first year of business, cost of goods sold starts with beginning inventory and is computed as follows:

Beginning inventory
+   Net purchases
Cost of goods available for sale
−   Ending inventory*
Cost of goods sold

* Based on the cost of the units purchased last.

PROBLEM 2: In 20X2, DuCo's second year of operations, it purchases merchandise on February 20 and August 9. Its inventory data for the year is as follows:

Purchase date	Number of units	Unit cost	Total cost
Beginning inventory..........	600*		$ 4,200
February 20................	2,100	$ 9	18,900
August 9	700	10	7,000

* 20X2 beginning inventory is the same as 20X1 ending inventory (computed in Solution 1)

DuCo's 20X2 year-end physical count shows 1,000 units on hand.
1. What is DuCo's goods available for sale in units and in dollars?
2. What is DuCo's ending inventory on December 31, 20X2?
3. What is its COGS for 20X2?

SOLUTION 2:

1. *To compute DuCo's 20X2 units available for sale:*

```
    600  beginning inventory
 +2,800* net units purchased
  3,400  units available for sale
```

```
*  2,100   February 20 purchase
 +  700    August 9 purchase
   2,800   net units purchased
```

To compute DuCo's 20X2 goods available for sale:

$ 4,200	beginning inventory (600 units x $7 per unit)
+25,900*	net purchases
$30,100	cost of goods available for sale

* $18,900	February 20 purchase (2,100 units x $9 per unit)
+ 7,000	August 9 purchase (700 units x $10 per unit)
$25,900	net purchases

2. To compute ending inventory:

FIFO costing assumes that the units in inventory at year end were the last units purchased (because the first units purchased were sold first). The physical count showed 1,000 units on hand, so you work backward, costing out the units in the last purchase, then the units in the next-to-last purchase, then the units in the purchase before that, and so on until the total number of units in ending inventory is reached. This is illustrated for DuCo as follows:

	Purchase date	Units	Unit cost	Total cost
From last purchase	August 9	700	$10	$7,000
From next-to-last purchase . . .	February 20	+ 300	9	+2,700
Total		1,000		$9,700

Once you know ending inventory, you can compute cost of goods sold.

3. To compute cost of goods sold, use the cost of goods sold schedule:

$ 4,200	beginning inventory (600 units x $7 per unit)
+25,900*	net purchases
$30,100	cost of goods available for sale
– 9,700	ending inventory
$20,400	**cost of goods sold in 20X2**

* Computed in Solution 2

To prove cost of goods sold: Start with the cost of units in beginning inventory, then cost out the units in the first purchase, the units in the second purchase and so on until you reach the total number of units sold during the year.

To illustrate:

Total units sold in 20X2: 2,400

Purchase date	Units sold	Unit cost	Total cost
From beginning inventory 600		$7	$ 4,200
From February 20 purchase . . . +1,800		9	+16,200
Total.................. 2,400		**COGS**	**$20,400**

PROBLEM 3: In 20X3, the company's third year of operation, DuCo makes two purchases:

Purchase date	Units purchased	Unit cost	Total cost
April 4 1,200		$14	$16,800
November 3............... +1,700		15	+25,500
Total 2,900			$42,300

The year-end physical count finds 1,300 units on hand.
1. How many units were available for sale during 20X3?
2. How many units did DuCo sell during 20X3?

SOLUTION 3:

1. *To compute units available for sale during 20X3:*

1,000	units in beginning inventory
+2,900	net purchases (see data in problem)
3,900	**units available for sale**

2. *To compute how many units DuCo sold during 20X3:*

3,900	units available for sale
−1,300	units in ending inventory
2,600	**units sold during 20X3**

PROBLEM 4: Use the data in Problem 3 to answer the following questions:

1. What is DuCo's ending inventory on its December 31, 20X3 balance sheet?
2. What is the COGS on its 20X3 income statement?

SOLUTION 4:

1. To compute DuCo's ending inventory on its December 31, 20X3 balance sheet:

1,300	units in ending inventory
x $15	per unit (November 3 purchase)
$19,500	ending inventory on DuCo's Dec. 31, 20X3 balance sheet

2. To compute DuCo's cost of goods sold on its 20X3 income statement:

$ 9,700	beginning inventory
+42,300*	net purchases
$52,000	cost of goods available for sale
–19,500	ending inventory
$32,500	cost of goods sold

*	$16,800	purchase on April 4 (1,200 units x $14 per unit)
*	+25,500	purchase on November 3 (1,700 units x $15 per unit)
*	$42,300	net purchases

To prove DuCo's cost of goods sold for 20X3:

Total units sold in 20X3: 2,600

Purchase date	Number of units	Unit cost	Total cost
Beginning inventory			
(From February 20, 20X2 purchase)....... 300		$ 9	$ 2,700
(From August 9, 20X2 purchase) 700		10	7,000
Units sold from April 4 purchase 1,200		14	16,800
Units sold from November 3 purchase .... + 400		15	+ 6,000
Total............................. 2,600		COGS	$32,500

Summary of FIFO Costing
Under the Periodic Method

The computation for ending inventory when FIFO costing is used under the periodic method is as follows:

Units on hand on Dec. 31 from most recent purchase X their unit cost
+ Units on hand on Dec. 31 from next most recent purchase X their unit cost
+ Units on hand on Dec. 31 from next most recent purchase X their unit cost
+ [etc, until total units in ending inventory are accounted for]
= Ending inventory

Cost of goods sold is always computed the same way under the periodic method, regardless of whether the costing method used is weighted average, FIFO, LIFO, or another method:

Beginning inventory
+   Net purchases
Cost of goods available for sale
−   Ending inventory
Cost of goods sold

To prove cost of goods sold, start with the cost of units in beginning inventory. (If beginning inventory contains more then one purchase from the previous year, start with the earliest one recorded, then add the cost of the next purchase included in beginning inventory, then the next, etc.) When all units in beginning inventory have been costed out, add the cost of units in the first purchase of the year, then the cost of units in the second purchase, then the third purchase, and so on until you reach total units sold for the year. In practice, adjustments are made for inventory lost to shrinkage.

FIFO Costing Under
the Perpetual Method

Under the perpetual method, the cost of goods sold is recorded for each sale at the time the sale is made:

Cash or Accounts Receivable	xxxx	
Sales Revenue		xxxx
Cost of Goods Sold	xxxx	
Inventory		xxxx

To compute cost of goods sold for a sale, start with the cost of units from beginning inventory (and within beginning inventory, start with the units from the earliest purchase recorded). Then cost out the units from the first purchase of the year, then those from the second purchase of the year and so on until the total number of units from the sale is reached.

In a company's first year of business, there is no beginning inventory, so start with the cost of units from the first purchase.

PROBLEM 5: FiCo begins operation in December, 20X6 and uses FIFO costing under the perpetual method. During 20X6, it makes the following merchandise purchases and sales for cash:

Purchase Date	Units purchased	Units sold	Unit cost	Unit sale price	Total cost	Total revenue
December 15....... 200			$0.90		$180	
December 20....... 100			1		100	
December 28.......		40		$2		$80

1. What are the journal entries for the purchases and sales?
2. What is FiCo's 20X6 ending inventory?
3. What is FiCo's 20X6 cost of goods sold?

SOLUTION 5: The easiest way to show how FIFO costing works under the perpetual method is to use the Inventory account.

Inventory Account									
	Purchases			**Sales**			**Balance**		
Date	**Units**	**Unit Cost**	**Total Cost**	**Units**	**Unit Cost**	**Total Cost**	**Units**	**Unit Cost**	**Total Cost**
December 15	200	0.90	180.00				200	0.90	180.00
December 20	100	1.00	100.00				200	0.90	180.00
							100	1.00	100.00
December 28				40	0.90	36.00	160	0.90	144.00
							100	1.00	100.00
Ending inventory									244.00
Cost of goods sold						36.00			

1. The journal entries for FiCo's 20X6 purchases and sales are:

For the December 15 purchase

Inventory	180	
Cash		180

(200 units x $.90 unit cost)

For the December 20 purchase

Inventory	100	
Cash		100

(100 units x $1 unit cost)

For the December 28 sale

Cash	80	
Sales Revenue		80

(40 units x $2 unit sales price)

Cost of Goods Sold	36*	
Inventory		36

(40 units x $.90 unit cost)

* Cost of goods sold is computed by starting with the earliest purchases in the year (first in) and working forward. The 40 units in this sale come from FiCo's first purchase (on December 15)

2. FiCo's 20X6 ending inventory, which may be found simply by looking at the balance in the Inventory account on December 31, is $244.

3. FiCo's 20X6 cost of goods sold is found by adding the cost of goods sold for all the sales during the year or simply checking the balance in Cost of Goods Sold. In 20X6, there was only one sale, so FiCo's cost of goods sold for the year is simply the cost of goods sold for the December 28 sale: $36.

PROBLEM 6: In 20X7, FiCo makes the following merchandise purchases and sales for cash:

20X7	Units Purchased	Units Sold	Unit Cost	Unit Sales Price	Total Cost	Total Revenue
February 4		60		$2.50		$ 150.00
March 9	400		$1.10		$440.00	
April 10		250		3.00		750.00
July 11	800		1.15		920.00	
August 17		450		3.50		1,575.00
December 20	300		1.20		360.00	

1. What are the journal entries for these purchases and sales?
2. What is FiCo's 20X7 ending inventory?
3. What is FiCo's 20X7 cost of goods sold?

SOLUTION 6: The Inventory account (page 110) shows the data for each journal entry, for ending inventory and for cost of goods sold. Remember that the *sale price* is applied only to sales revenue—it has no bearing on the cost of goods sold.

1. The journal entries for FiCo's 20X7 purchases and sales are:

<u>For the February 4 sale</u>

Cash	150	
Sales Revenue		150

(60 units x $2.50 unit sale price)

Cost of Goods Sold	54*	
Inventory		54

(60 units x $.90 unit cost)

* Cost of goods sold is computed by starting with beginning inventory and working forward. For the February 4 sale, the 60 units are costed out from the first portion of FiCo's beginning inventory—from the 160 units. To compute:
60 units from first part of beginning inventory x $.90 unit cost = $54 COGS

	Purchases			Sales			Balance		
Date	**Units**	**Unit Cost**	**Total Cost**	**Units**	**Unit Cost**	**Total Cost**	**Units**	**Unit Cost**	**Total Cost**
20X6									
December 15	200	0.90	180.00				200	0.90	180.00
December 20	100	1.00	100.00				200	0.90	180.00
							100	1.00	100.00
December 28				40	0.90	36.00	160	0.90	144.00
							100	1.00	100.00
Ending inventory									244.00
Cost of goods sold						36.00			
20X7									
January 1							160	0.90	144.00
(Beginning inventory)							100	1.00	100.00
February 4				60	0.90	54.00	100	0.90	90.00
							100	1.00	100.00
March 9	400	1.10	440.00				100	0.90	90.00
							100	1.00	100.00
							400	1.10	440.00
April 10				100	0.90	90.00			
				100	1.00	100.00			
				50	1.10	55.00	350	1.10	385.00
July 11	800	1.15	920.00				350	1.10	385.00
							800	1.15	920.00
August 17				350	1.10	385.00			
				100	1.15	115.00	700	1.15	805.00
December 20	300	1.20	360.00				700	1.15	805.00
							300	1.20	360.00
Ending Inventory									1,165.00
Cost of goods sold						799.00			

For the March 9 purchase
Inventory   440
    Cash   440
(400 units x $1.10 unit cost)

For the April 10 sale
Cash   750
    Sales Revenue   750
(250 units x $3 unit sales price)

Cost of Goods Sold   245*
    Inventory   245

* Total units sold on April 10: 250

	Units sold	Unit cost	Total cost
Units from beginning inventory (January 1)	100*	$0.90	$ 90
	100	1.00	100
Units from first 20X7 purchase (March 9)	+50	1.10	+ 55
Total	250	**COGS**	**$245**

* There are only 100 units left at $.90 per unit in beginning inventory because 60 units were costed out in the February 4 sale (160 units – 60 units = 100 units)

For the July 11 purchase
Inventory   920
    Cash   920
(800 units x $1.15)

For the August 17 sale
Cash   1,575
    Sales Revenue   1,575
(450 units x $3.50 unit sales price)

Cost of Goods Sold   500*
    Inventory   500
* Total units sold on August 17: 450

	Units sold	Unit cost	Total cost
Units from the second 20X7 purchase (March 9) ..	350	$1.10	$385
Units from third 20X7 purchase (July 11)	100	1.15	115
Total................................	450	**COGS**	**$500**

<u>For the December 20 purchase</u>

Inventory	360	
Cash		360

(300 units x $1.20)

2. FiCo's 20X7 ending inventory may be found simply by looking at the inventory balance on December 31: $1,165.

3. FiCo's 20X7 cost of goods sold may be found by adding up the cost of goods sold for all the sales made in 20X7: $799. It may also be found simply by looking at the balance in the Cost of Goods Sold account.

Ending Inventory and COGS Are the Same under the Periodic and Perpetual Methods

Ending inventory and cost of goods sold were computed above using FIFO costing under the perpetual method. Below, they are computed using FIFO costing under the periodic method. Note that the results are the same and that either amount may also be found by looking at the balance in the Cost of Goods Sold account.

To compute FiCo's cost of goods sold for 20X6 using the periodic method:

	Units	Cost
Net purchases*	300	$280
– Ending inventory	–260	–244
Cost of goods sold	40	$ 36

* Same as cost of goods available for sale in a company's first year of business

To compute FiCo's cost of goods sold for 20X7 using the periodic method:

$ 244	beginning inventory
+1,720*	net purchases
$1,964	cost of goods available for sale
–1,165	ending inventory
$ 799	**cost of goods sold**

* $ 440	purchase on March 9 (400 units x $1.10 per unit)
920	purchase on July 11 (800 units x $1.15 per unit)
360	purchase on December 20 (300 units x $1.20 per unit)
$1,720	net purchases

Income Tax Consequences

FIFO costing relies on the oldest purchases to calculate cost of goods sold. Therefore, when prices are rising, the cost of units purchased at the beginning of the year are lower than those purchased at the end of the year, so FIFO will produce a lower cost of goods sold, resulting in both higher income and income taxes.

QUIZ 1   INVENTORY COSTING USING THE FIFO METHOD

Note: Arrows used in the Inventory accounts in the solutions are for illustrative purposes only and should not appear in your answers.

Problem I.

HuCo begins operation in October, 20X1 and makes the following purchases and sales:

Purchase date	Units purchased	Unit cost
November 4	1,200	$4
December 11	2,300	6

The year-end physical count shows 700 units on hand. HuCo uses the periodic method and FIFO costing.

1. What is its ending inventory on December 31, 20X1?

2. What is its 20X1 cost of goods sold?

Problem II.

SoCo has 2,000 units in ending inventory on December 31, 20X7 at $4 per unit. SoCo makes three purchases during 20X8:

Purchase Date	Units purchased	Unit cost
March 10	1,700	$ 6
August 4.	1,900	10
November 20	3,500	9

On December 31, 20X8, SoCo has 1,500 units in ending inventory. If SoCo uses FIFO costing and the periodic method, what is its cost of goods sold for 20X8?

Problem III.

LoCo opens for business during 20X2 and makes the following transactions:

Purchase date	Units purchased	Units sold	Unit cost	Unit sale price
August 3............400			$5	
September 19........700			7	
October 22 600			8	
November 12		1,300		$16
December 3 700			9	

LoCo uses FIFO costing and the perpetual method.

1. What is LoCo's ending inventory on its December 31, 20X2 balance sheet?

2. What is LoCo's cost of goods sold on its 20X2 income statement?

Fill in the blank Inventory account with each amount given and each amount that you compute.

Inventory Account									
	Purchases			**Sales**			**Balance**		
Date	Units	Unit Cost	Total Cost	Units	Unit Cost	Total Cost	Units	Unit Cost	Total Cost
Ending inventory									
Cost of goods sold									

Problem IV.

NeCo's records show the following data:

Date	Units purchased	Units sold	Unit cost
20X6			
November 15	800		$ 4
December 4	200		6
20X7			
January 1	1,000		
(beginning inventory)			
January 15		950	
March 14	2,300		$ 9
June 25		1,000	
August 10	3,600		13
October 29		3,100	

NeCo uses FIFO costing and the perpetual method. What is the cost of goods sold for its January, June and October sales? Use the inventory account on below to find and show the answers.

Inventory Account									
	Purchases			**Sales**			**Balance**		
Date	**Units**	**Unit Cost**	**Total Cost**	**Units**	**Unit Cost**	**Total Cost**	**Units**	**Unit Cost**	**Total Cost**
20X6									
Ending inventory									
20X7									
January 1 (Beginning inventory)									

Problem V.

RaCo, which uses FIFO costing and the periodic method, computed cost of goods sold for the year at $154,000. You are asked to prove this amount based on the following data:

Beginning inventory: 1,200 units at $15 per unit.

Purchase date	Units purchased	Unit cost	Total cost
February 1.	3,000	$18	$ 54,000
June 10	4,000	19	76,000
August 15	2,000	20	40,000
November 8.	+ 2,800	23	+ 64,400
Net purchases.	11,800		$234,400

A physical count of ending inventory showed 4,500 units.

$ 18,000	beginning inventory (1,200 x $15)
+234,400	net purchases
$252,400	cost of goods available for sale
– 98,400	ending inventory
$154,000	cost of goods sold

QUIZ 1 Solutions and Explanations

Problem I.

1. *To compute HuCo's ending inventory:*

700	units on hand at year end
x $ 6	unit cost of purchase closest to year end
$4,200	**ending inventory**

2. *To compute HuCo's cost of goods sold:*

	Units	Cost
Net purchases	3,500	$18,600*
– Ending inventory	– 700	– 4,200
Cost of goods sold	2,800	$14,400

* $ 4,800	purchase on November 4 (1,200 units x $4 per unit)
+13,800	purchase on December 11 (2,300 units x $6 per unit)
$18,600	net purchases

Problem II.

To compute SoCo's cost of goods sold:

	Units	Cost
Beginning inventory	2,000	$ 8,000
+ Net purchases	+7,100	+60,700*
Goods available for sale	9,100	$68,700
– Ending inventory	–1,500	–13,500**
Cost of goods sold	7,600	**$55,200**

* $10,200	purchase on March 10 (1,700 units x $6 per unit)
19,000	purchase on August 4 (1,900 units x $10 per unit)
+31,500	purchase on November 20 (3,500 x $9 per unit)
$60,700	net purchases.

** To derive ending inventory using FIFO, you start with the cost of units in the last purchase made, add the cost of units in the next-to-last purchase, then the cost of units in the purchase before that, and so on. In this case, there are 1,500 units in ending inventory, and the last purchase was for 3,500 units. Thus, all the units in ending inventory are from this purchase.

Problem III.

Your completed Inventory account showing LoCo's 20X2 ending inventory and cost of goods sold should appear as follows:

Inventory Account										
	Purchases			**Sales**			**Balance**			
Date	Units	Unit Cost	Total Cost	Units	Unit Cost	Total Cost	Units	Unit Cost	Total Cost	
August 3	400	5.00	2,000.00				400	5.00	2,000.00	
September 19	700	7.00	4,900.00				400	5.00	2,000.00	
							700	7.00	4,900.00	
October 22	600	8.00	4,800.00				400	5.00	2,000.00	
							700	7.00	4,900.00	
							600	8.00	4,800.00	
November 12				400	5.00	2,000.00				
				700	7.00	4,900.00				
				200	8.00	1,600.00	400	8.00	3,200.00	
December 3	700	9.00	6,300.00				400	8.00	3,200.00	
							700	9.00	6,300.00	
Ending Inventory									9,500.00	
Cost of goods sold						8,500.00				

As the Inventory account above shows:

1. LoCo's ending inventory on its December 31, 20X2 balance sheet is $9,500.

2. LoCo's cost of goods sold on its December 31, 20X2 income statement is $8,500.

Problem IV.

The completed Inventory account showing NeCo's cost of goods sold for its January, June and October sales should appear as follows:

Inventory Account										
	Purchases			Sales			Balance			
Date	Units	Unit Cost	Total Cost	Units	Unit Cost	Total Cost	Units	Unit Cost	Total Cost
20X6									
November 15	800	4.00	3,200.00				800	4.00	3,200.00
December 4	200	6.00	1,200.00				800	4.00	3,200.00
							200	6.00	1,200.00
Ending inventory									4,400.00
20X7									
January 1 (Beginning inventory)							800	4.00	3,200.00
							200	6.00	1,200.00
January 15				800	4.00	3,200.00			
				150	6.00	900.00	50	6.00	300.00
March 14	2,300	9.00	20,700.00				50	6.00	300.00
							2,300	9.00	20,700.00
June 25				50	6.00	300.00			
				950	9.00	8,550.00	1,350	9.00	12,150.00
August 10	3,600	13.00	46,800.00				1,350	9.00	12,150.00
							3,600	13.00	46,800.00
October 29				1,350	9.00	12,150.00			
				1,750	13.00	22,750.00	1,850	13.00	24,050.00

As the Inventory account above shows:
The cost of goods sold for the January sale is: $4,100 ($3,200 + $900)

The cost of goods sold for the June sale is: $8,850 ($300 + $8,550)

The cost of goods sold for the October sale is: $34,900 ($12,150 + $22,750).

Problem V.

To prove RaCo's cost of goods sold, the first step is to find the number of units sold during the year:

1,200	units in beginning inventory
+11,800	units purchased
13,000	units available for sale
– 4,500	units in ending inventory
8,500	units sold during the year

Total units sold: 8,500

Purchase Date	Units	Unit cost	Total cost
Beginning inventory	1,200	$15	$ 18,000
Units sold from February 1 purchase . . .	3,000	18	54,000
Units sold from June 10 purchase	4,000	19	76,000
Units sold from August 15 purchase . . .	+300*	20	+ 6,000
Total	8,500	**COGS**	**$154,000**

* Although the August 15 purchase was for 2,000 units, you need only 300 units from this purchase to arrive at the total of 8,500 units sold for the year. For the same reason, you do not need to cost out any units from the November 8 purchase.

QUIZ 2   INVENTORY COSTING USING THE FIFO METHOD

Problem I.

TaCo begins operation during 20X1 and records the following data:

Purchase date	Units purchased	Units sold	Unit cost	Unit sales price
November 14	1,000 on account		$30	
December 2	1,500 for cash		33	
December 18		2,100		$45

The December 18 sale was on account. TaCo uses FIFO costing and the perpetual method.

1. Prepare the journal entries TaCo must record for 20X1. Use the inventory account below to find and show the amounts used in the entries. (*Hint:* Not all the computations needed for the journal entries will be in the inventory account.)

2. Prove cost of goods sold for the December 18 sale.

		Inventory Account								
	Purchases			**Sales**			**Balance**			
Date	Units	Unit Cost	Total Cost	Units	Unit Cost	Total Cost	Units	Unit Cost	Total Cost	
Ending inventory										
Cost of goods sold										

Problem II.

VuCo uses FIFO costing and the perpetual method. It shows the following data for 20X2 and 20X3:

20X2	Units Purchased	Units Sold	Unit Cost
December 2	1,800		$6.00
December 5	1,100		8.00
December 10		1,500	

20X3	Units Purchased	Units Sold	Unit Cost
Beginning Inventory	1,400		
January 13		1,000	
February 14	3,600		$ 9.00
March 30	2,800		13.00
July 31		2,900	

Use the inventory account on page 124 to find and show the following amounts.

1. What is VuCo's ending inventory on December 31, 20X3?

2. What is its 20X3 cost of goods sold?

	Inventory Account								
	Purchases			**Sales**			**Balance**		
Date	Units	Unit Cost	Total Cost	Units	Unit Cost	Total Cost	Units	Unit Cost	Total Cost
20X2									
Ending inventory									
20X3									
Ending Inventory									
Cost of goods sold									

Problem III.

RiCo opens in 20X5 and makes the following purchases and sales:

Date	Purchases	Sales
July 24.	400 units @ $10	
August 4.	600 units @ $12	
September 19 . .		500 units @ $20
October 10. . . .	900 units @ $15	
November 3 . . .	1,100 units @ $17	
December 1 . . .		800 units @ $26

RiCo uses the perpetual method and FIFO costing. What is RiCo's ending inventory on its December 31, 20X5 balance sheet? Use the inventory account below to find and show the ending inventory amount.

	Inventory Account								
	Purchases			**Sales**			**Balance**		
Date	Units	Unit Cost	Total Cost	Units	Unit Cost	Total Cost	Units	Unit Cost	Total Cost
Ending inventory									

Problem IV.

MaCo shows the following data for 20X3 and 20X4:

20X3	Units Purchased	Units Sold	Unit Cost
December 4	600		$12.00
December 21	1,100		14.00
December 22		200	

20X4	Units Purchased	Units Sold	Unit Cost
January 1 (Beginning Inventory)	1,500		
May 27	3,300		$17.00
August 14		500	
October 22	1,000		21.00
November 1		3,200	
November 30		900	
Ending inventory	1,200		

Inventory Account									
	Purchases			Sales			Balance		
Date	Units	Unit Cost	Total Cost	Units	Unit Cost	Total Cost	Units	Unit Cost	Total Cost
20X3									
Ending inventory									
20X4									
January 1 (Beginning inventory)									
Ending Inventory Cost of goods sold									

Use the inventory account above to find and show the following amounts for both questions.

1. What is MaCo's ending inventory on its December 31, 20X4 balance sheet?

2. What is MaCo's cost of goods sold on its 20X4 income statement?

Problem V.

Use the following information to answer the three questions that follow. Apply FIFO costing and the periodic method.

Purchase date	20X2 Purchases	20X3 Purchases
February.	400 @ $2	600 @ $ 6
June	800 @ $4	900 @ $10
October	1,000 @ $5	800 @ $12

1. During 20X2, 1,500 units are sold. Calculate the 20X2 cost of goods sold.

2. On December 31, 20X2 there are 700 units in ending inventory. On December 31, 20X3 there are 300 units in ending inventory. What is ending inventory on the December 31, 20X3 balance sheet?

3. What is the cost of goods sold on the 20X3 income statement?

QUIZ 2   Solutions and Explanations

Problem I.

	Inventory Account									
	Purchases			Sales			Balance			
Date	Units	Unit Cost	Total Cost	Units	Unit Cost	Total Cost	Units	Unit Cost	Total Cost	
November 14	1,000	30.00	30,000.00				1,000	30.00	30,000.00	
December 2	1,500	33.00	49,500.00				1,000	30.00	30,000.00	
							1,500	33.00	49,500.00	
December 18				1,000	30.00	30,000.00				
				1,100	33.00	36,300.00	400	33.00	13,200.00	
Ending inventory									13,200.00	
Cost of goods sold						66,300.00				

1. The journal entries that TaCo must record in 20X1 are:

<u>For November 14 purchase</u>
Inventory	30,000	
Accounts Payable		30,000

(1,000 units x $30 unit cost)

<u>For the December 2 purchase</u>
Inventory	49,500	
Cash		49,500

(1,500 units x $33 unit cost)

<u>For the December 18 sale</u>
Accounts Receivable	94,500	
Sales Revenue		94,500

(2,100 units sold x $45 unit sales price)

Cost of Goods Sold	66,300*	
Inventory		66,300

* To prove cost of goods sold for the December 18 sale, see number 2 that follows.

2. To prove cost of goods sold for the December 18 sale:

Total units sold in 20X1: 2,100

Purchase date	Units sold	Unit cost	Total cost
Units sold from November 14 purchase. . .	1,000	$30	$30,000
Units sold from December 2 purchase . .	+1,100	33	+36,300
Total	2,100	COGS	$66,300

Problem II.

	Inventory Account								
	Purchases			**Sales**			**Balance**		
Date	**Units**	**Unit Cost**	**Total Cost**	**Units**	**Unit Cost**	**Total Cost**	**Units**	**Unit Cost**	**Total Cost**
20X2									
December 2	1,800	6.00	10,800.00				1,800	6.00	10,800.00
December 5	1,100	8.00	8,800.00				1,800	6.00	10,800.00
							1,100	8.00	8,800.00
December 10				1,500	6.00	9,000.00	300	6.00	1,800.00
							1,100	8.00	8,800.00
Ending inventory									10,600.00
20X3									
January 1 (Beginning inventory)							300	6.00	1,800.00
							1,100	8.00	8,800.00
January 13				300	6.00	1,800.00			
				700	8.00	5,600.00	400	8.00	3,200.00
February 14	3,600	9.00	32,400.00				400	8.00	3,200.00
							3,600	9.00	32,400.00
March 30	2,800	13.00	36,400.00				400	8.00	3,200.00
							3,600	9.00	32,400.00
							2,800	13.00	36,400.00
July 31				400	8.00	3,200.00			
				2,500	9.00	22,500.00	1,100	9.00	9,900.00
							2,800	13.00	36,400.00
Ending Inventory									46,300.00
Cost of goods sold						33,100.00			

As the Inventory account above shows:

1. VuCo's ending inventory on December 31, 20X3 is $46,300.

2. VuCo's 20X3 cost of goods sold is $33,100.

Problem III.

Inventory Account										
	Purchases			**Sales**			**Balance**			
Date	**Units**	**Unit Cost**	**Total Cost**	**Units**	**Unit Cost**	**Total Cost**	**Units**	**Unit Cost**	**Total Cost**	
July 24	400	10.00	4,000.00				400	10.00	4,000.00	
August 4	600	12.00	7,200.00				400	10.00	4,000.00	
							600	12.00	7,200.00	
September 19				400	10.00	4,000.00				
				100	12.00	1,200.00	500	12.00	6,000.00	
October 10	900	15.00	13,500.00				500	12.00	6,000.00	
							900	15.00	13,500.00	
November 3	1,100	17.00	18,700.00				500	12.00	6,000.00	
							900	15.00	13,500.00	
							1,100	17.00	18,700.00	
December 1				500	12.00	6,000.00				
				300	15.00	4,500.00	600	15.00	9,000.00	
							1,100	17.00	18,700.00	
Ending Inventory									27,700.00	

As the Inventory account above shows, RiCo's ending inventory on December 31, 20X5 is $27,700.

Problem IV.

Inventory Account									
	Purchases			**Sales**			**Balance**		
Date	**Units**	**Unit Cost**	**Total Cost**	**Units**	**Unit Cost**	**Total Cost**	**Units**	**Unit Cost**	**Total Cost**
20X3									
December 4	600	12.00	7,200.00				600	12.00	7,200.00
December 21	1,100	14.00	15,400.00				600	12.00	7,200.00
							1,100	14.00	15,400.00
December 22				200	12.00	2,400.00	400	12.00	4,800.00
							1,100	14.00	15,400.00
Ending inventory									20,200.00
20X4									
January 1 (Beginning inventory)							400	12.00	4,800.00
							1,100	14.00	15,400.00
May 27	3,300	17.00	56,100.00				400	12.00	4,800.00
							1,100	14.00	15,400.00
							3,300	17.00	56,100.00
August 14				400	12.00	4,800.00			
				100	14.00	1,400.00	1,000	14.00	14,000.00
							3,300	17.00	56,100.00
October 22	1,000	21.00	21,000.00				1,000	14.00	14,000.00
							3,300	17.00	56,100.00
							1,000	21.00	21,000.00
November 1				1,000	14.00	14,000.00			
				2,200	17.00	37,400.00	1,100	17.00	18,700.00
							1,000	21.00	21,000.00
November 30				900	17.00	15,300.00	200	17.00	3,400.00
							1,000	21.00	21,000.00
									24,400.00
Ending Inventory Cost of goods sold						72,900.00			

As the Inventory account above shows:

1. MaCo's ending inventory on its December 31, 20X4 balance sheet is $24,400.

2. MaCo's 20X4 cost of goods sold is $72,900.

Problem V.

To answer the first question, apply the format that is used to prove cost of goods sold.

1. *To compute 20X2 cost of goods sold:*

Total units sold in 20X2: 1,500

Purchase date	Units sold	Unit cost	Total cost
Units sold from February purchase	400	$2	$ 800
Units sold from June purchase.	800	4	3,200
Units sold from October purchase	+ 300	5	+1,500
Total	1,500	**COGS**	**$5,500**

2. *To find the cost of ending inventory:* Start with the cost of units in the last purchase, then go to the cost of units in the next-to-last purchase, then the cost of units in the purchase before that, and so on. In this case, however, all the units are from the last (October, 20X3) purchase, so the computation is simple.

300	units in ending inventory (given in the data)
x $ 12	per unit (from the last purchase of the year in October)
$3,600	ending inventory

3. *To compute 20X3 cost of goods sold:*

$ 3,500	beginning inventory (700 units x $5 per unit)
+22,200*	net purchases
$25,700	cost of goods available for sale
– 3,600	ending inventory
$22,100	cost of goods sold

* To compute net purchases:

$ 3,600	February purchase (600 units x $6 per unit)
9,000	June purchase (900 units x $10 per unit)
+ 9,600	October purchase (800 units x $12 per unit)
$22,200	net purchases

INVENTORY COSTING USING THE LIFO METHOD

Introduction

Because last-in-first-out (LIFO) costing is used most often with the periodic method, that is what this course covers. Note this distinction from FIFO and average costing (weighted average and moving average), both of which are regularly used with the periodic or perpetual methods.

How to Use LIFO Costing

LIFO does not precisely match revenue from sales with the actual cost of the merchandise sold. Instead, it is based on the assumption that the last units a company purchased ("last in") were the first units it sold ("first out").

Computing Ending Inventory Under LIFO

When a physical count of ending inventory is taken at year end, it is assumed that the units on hand were the first units purchased. Thus, *to cost out ending inventory, start with the cost of the units purchased first and continue to cost out units in the order in which they were purchased until you reach total units in ending inventory.*

Computing Cost of Goods Sold (COGS) Under LIFO

To compute COGS under LIFO, simply use the cost of goods sold schedule:

Beginning inventory
+ Net purchases
Cost of goods available for sale
− Ending inventory
Cost of goods sold

EXAMPLE 1: LiCo started up in December, 20X0 and made the following purchases:

Purchase date	Units purchased	Unit cost	Total cost
December 15	100	$3	$ 300
December 17	70	4	280
December 19	+150	5	+ 750
Total	320		$1,330

At year-end 20X0, a physical count of inventory shows 150 units on hand. Using LIFO costing, what is LiCo's ending inventory? What is its cost of goods sold?

To compute ending inventory: Start by costing out units from LiCo's first purchase of the year, then its second purchase, and so on until you reach the 150 units in ending inventory, as follows

Total units in 20X0 ending inventory: 150

	Purchase date	Units sold	Unit cost	Total cost
From first purchase	December 15	100	$3	$300
From second purchase	December 17	+ 50	4	+200
Total		150	**Ending inventory**	$500

To compute cost of goods sold: Use the cost of goods sold statement:

$ 0	beginning inventory in 20X0
1,330	net purchases
$1,330	available for sale (same as purchases in the company's first year)
– 500	ending inventory
$ 830	cost of goods sold in 20X0

To prove cost of goods sold: First, find out how many units were sold during the year:

320	units available for sale (same as units purchased in the first year)
–150	units in ending inventory
170	units sold in 20X0

Because the units *last in* were those *first out*, cost out the 170 units sold by starting with the last purchase and working backward. Add the cost of units in the next-to-last purchase, then the purchase before that and so on until you reach total units sold.

Total units sold in 20X1: 170

	Purchase date	Units sold	Unit cost	Total cost
From last purchase	December 19	150	$5	$750
From next-to-last purchase . .	December 17	+ 20	4	+ 80
Total		170	**COGS**	**$830**

This method of costing out merchandise sold for the year can also be used when you need to know COGS before you know ending inventory.

LIFO Layers

Each year in which a company buys more units than it sells, a *LIFO layer* is created. In a company's first year, ending inventory becomes the LIFO layer.

From the second year on, each year's LIFO layer may be computed in one of two ways:

Units found in year-end physical count
<u>– Units in beginning inventory</u>
Units in LIFO layer for the year

or

<u>Total units purchased</u>
<u>–   Total units sold</u>
Units in LIFO layer for the year

To cost out the new LIFO layer, start with the unit cost of the first purchase of the year, then add the cost of units in the order in which you purchased them until you reach the required number of units. After several years, beginning and ending inventory may comprise several layers.

> **EXAMPLE 2:** DuCo begins operations in October, 20X1 and makes one purchase—on November 8, it buys 900 units at $3 each. At year end, DuCo's physical count of inventory shows 500 units. 1. What is DuCo's 20X1 ending inventory? 2. What is its 20X1 inventory layer? 3. What is its 20X1 cost of goods sold?
>
> 1. *To compute ending inventory:* 500 units on hand x $3 per unit = $1,500 ending inventory.

To compute DuCo's 20X1 inventory layer: In a company's first year, ending inventory becomes the inventory layer; for DuCo, it is $1,500.

To compute DuCo's 20X1 cost of goods sold: Use the cost of goods sold schedule:

$ 0	beginning inventory in 20X1
+2,700	net purchases (900 units x $3 per unit)
$2,700	available for sale (same as purchases in the company's first year)
–1,500	ending inventory
$1,200	cost of goods sold in 20X1

EXAMPLE 3: In 20X2, DuCo shows the following data:

Purchase date	Units	Unit cost	Total cost
20X1 LIFO layer	500	$3	$ 1,500
March 6 purchase	700	$4	$ 2,800
July 17 purchase.	900	6	5,400
November 4 purchase	+1,200	7	+ 8,400
Total purchases	2,800		$16,600

At year end, a physical count shows 600 units on hand. 1. What is DuCo's 20X2 LIFO layer? 2. What is its 20X2 ending inventory? 3. What is its 20X2 cost of goods sold?

1. *To compute DuCo's 20X2 LIFO layer:*

600	units found in 20X2 year-end physical count
–500	units in 20X2 beginning inventory (equal to 20X1 ending inventory)
100	units in 20X2 LIFO layer

To compute the cost of DuCo's 20X2 LIFO layer, cost out units in the order they were purchased. Because DuCo's 20X2 LIFO layer is only 100 units, you can cost it out from the first purchase on March 6 at $4 per unit:

100 units in 20X2 LIFO layer x $4 per unit = $400 LIFO layer for 20X2.

2. *To compute DuCo's 20X2 ending inventory:* Add the 20X1 and 20X2 LIFO layers:

20X1 LIFO layer
  units   500
  x unit cost x $ 3
  total cost $1,500

20X2 LIFO layer:
  units   100
  x unit cost x $ 4
  total cost   + 400
20X2 ending inventory $1,900

3. *To compute DuCo's 20X2 cost of goods sold:* Use the cost of goods sold schedule:

$ 1,500	beginning inventory in 20X2 (same as 20X1 ending inventory)
+16,600	net purchases
$18,100	available for sale
– 1,900	ending inventory
$16,200	cost of goods sold in 20X2

To prove DuCo's 20X2 cost of goods sold: The first step is compute the number of units that DuCo sold in 20X2:

To compute units sold in 20X2:

500	units in 20X2 beginning inventory (from the 20X1 LIFO layer)
+2,800	net units purchased
3,300	units available for sale
– 600	units in ending inventory
2,700	units sold in 20X2

Because LIFO assumes that the units *last in* were the ones *first out*, start with the cost of the units in the last purchase of the year and work backward. Add the cost of units in the next-to-last purchase, the cost of units in the purchase before that and so on.

Total units sold in 20X2: 2,700

	Purchase date	Units sold	Unit cost	Total cost
From last purchase	November 4	1,200	$7	$ 8,400
From next-to-last purchase . .	July 17	900	6	5,400
From third-to-last purchase . .	March 6	+ 600	4	+ 2,400
Total		2,700	**COGS**	**$16,200**

Note: If you need to cost out merchandise sold (that is, to compute COGS) before year end, you can use this method.

The following problems and solutions illustrate how LIFO layers are created through the continuing example of WiCo.

PROBLEM 1: WiCo opens for business in 20X4 and makes the following purchases:

Purchase date	Units purchased	Unit cost	Total cost
May 12	600	$11	$ 6,600
October 1	+2,200	14	+30,800
Total	2,800*		$37,400*

* In the company's first year, total purchases are the same as total available for sale.

On December 31, 20X4, a physical count of inventory finds 1,000 units on hand. If WiCo uses LIFO costing under the periodic method, what is its ending inventory on December 31, 20X4? What is its 20X4 LIFO layer?

SOLUTION 1: *To compute ending inventory under LIFO,* cost out units in the order they were purchased until you reach total units in ending inventory:

Total units in 20X4 ending inventory : 1,000

	Purchase date	Units purchased	Unit cost	Total cost
From first purchase	May 12	600	$11	$ 6,600
From second purchase.	October 1	+ 400	14	+ 5,600
20X4 LIFO layer (ending inventory)		1,000		$12,200

WiCo's 20X4 ending inventory and LIFO layer is $12,200.

PROBLEM 2: Using the information in Problem 1, what is WiCo's 20X4 cost of goods sold?

SOLUTION 2: *To compute WiCo's COGS,* use the cost of goods sold schedule:

$ 0	beginning inventory in 20X4
+ 37,400	net purchases
$ 37,400	available for sale
– 12,200	ending inventory
$ 25,200	cost of goods sold in 20X4

PROBLEM 3: Prove that WiCo's 20X4 cost of goods sold is $25,200.

SOLUTION 3: *First, compute how many units WiCo sold in 20X4:*

0	units in beginning inventory
+2,800	net units purchased
2,800	units available for sale
−1,000	units in ending inventory
1,800	units sold in 20X4

To prove COGS under LIFO: Cost out units starting with the last purchase of the year and work backward. Add the cost of units in the next-to-last purchase, in the purchase before that and so on until you reach total units sold. WiCo's last purchase of 2,200 units on October 1 was large enough to reach total units sold of 1,800 units:

1,800 units x $14 per unit = $25,200 cost of goods sold in 20X4.

PROBLEM 4: In 20X5, WiCo shows the following data:

Purchase date	Units	Unit cost	Total cost
20X4 LIFO layer	1,000		$12,200
April 10 purchase	900	$18	$16,200
November 22 purchase	+2,200	20	+44,000
Total purchases	3,100		$60,200

At year end, a physical count finds 1,300 units in ending inventory. How many units are in WiCo's 20X5 LIFO layer?

SOLUTION 4: *To compute:*

1,300	units in 20X5 found in year-end physical count
−1,000	units in beginning inventory (same as 20X4 ending inventory)
300	units in 20X5 LIFO layer

The first purchase of 900 units on April 1 is large enough to cost out the 300 units in WiCo's 20X5 LIFO layer:

300 units x $18 per unit = $5,400 cost of 20X5 LIFO layer.

PROBLEM 5: Using the information in Problems 1 and 4, cost out WiCo's 20X5 ending inventory.

SOLUTION 5: *To compute:*

Units	Unit cost	Total Cost	LIFO layer
20X4 LIFO layer			
600	$11	$6,600	
400	14	+5,600	$12,200
20X5 LIFO layer			
300	18	$5,400	+ 5,400
20X5 ending inventory			$17,600

PROBLEM 6: Using the information in Problems 4 and 5, what is WiCo's 20X5 cost of goods sold?

SOLUTION 6: *To compute, using the cost of goods sold statement:*

$12,200	beginning inventory in 20X5 (same as 20X4 ending inventory)
+60,200	net purchases
$72,400	available for sale
−17,600	ending inventory
$54,800	cost of goods sold in 20X5

PROBLEM 7: How do you prove WiCo's 20X5 cost of goods sold of $54,800?

SOLUTION 7: *To compute how many units WiCo sold in 20X5:*

1,000	units in 20X5 beginning inventory (same as 20X4 ending inventory)
+3,100	net units purchased
4,100	units available for sale
−1,300	units in ending inventory
2,800	units sold in 20X5

To compute COGS under LIFO, cost out the units starting with the last purchase of the year and work backward. Add the cost of units in the next-to-last purchase, the purchase before that and so on until you reach total units sold.

Total units sold in 20X5: 2,800

	Purchase date	Units sold	Unit cost	Total cost
From last purchase	November 22	2,200	$20	$44,000
From next-to-last purchase . .	April 10	+ 600	18	+10,800
Total		2,800	**COGS**	**$54,800**

Because 3,100 units were purchased in 20X5 and 2,800 units were sold, 300 units will remain in ending inventory and become the 20X5 LIFO layer. These 300 units are from the April 10 purchase.

Note: If you need to cost out merchandise sold (that is, to compute COGS) before year end, you can use this method.

Summary of Costing Out Ending Inventory Under LIFO

Under LIFO, ending inventory is costed out as follows:

In a company's first year, ending inventory becomes the LIFO (or inventory) layer. To cost out this layer, start with the cost of units from the first purchase of the year and continue to cost out units in the order they were purchased until you reach total units in ending inventory.

In a company's second year and in subsequent years, if units purchased exceed units sold, compute each year's LIFO layer as follows:

Units found in year-end physical count
– Units in beginning inventory
Units in LIFO layer for the year

Once you know the number of units in the LIFO layer for a given year, compute the layer by costing out units in the order they were purchased.

After you cost out the LIFO layer for the year, add that amount to previous LIFO layers. After several years, ending inventory may have many such layers.

To find COGS under LIFO, use the cost of goods sold schedule:

Beginning inventory
+ Net purchases
Cost of goods available for sale
– Ending inventory
Cost of goods sold

To prove COGS, or to find COGS when you do not know the cost of ending inventory, compute total units sold during the year. Then cost out the units sold starting with the last purchase of the year and work backward, costing out units in the next-to-last purchase, the purchase before that and so on until total units sold are reached.

LIFO Liquidation

As noted above, when a company buys more units in a year than it sells, a LIFO layer is created. When it *sells* more units than it *buys*, part or all of a LIFO layer, or of several layers, are *liquidated* or used up to cost out the goods sold. They are liquidated in reverse order: first you liquidate the prior year's LIFO layer, then the layer from the year before that and so on until you have costed out all units sold.

EXAMPLE 4: In 20X4, HaCo purchases 5,000 units at $6 each and sells 6,000 units. HaCo's records show the following data:

Year	Units purchased	Unit cost	Total cost
20X1 LIFO layer	400	$2	$ 800
20X2 LIFO layer	500	3	1,500
20X3 LIFO layer	+ 700	5	+ 3,500
20X4 beginning inventory . . .	1,600		$ 5,800
20X4 purchases	5,000	$6	$30,000

To cost out HaCo's 2004 COGS:

Total units sold in 20X4: 6,000

Year	Units sold	Unit cost	Total cost
20X4 purchases	5,000	$6	$30,000
20X3 LIFO layer	700	5	3,500
20X2 LIFO layer	+ 300	3	+ 900
Total	6,000		**COGS** $34,400

Once current purchases are exhausted, you invade (cost out units from) beginning inventory to cost out sales. The last LIFO layer is liquidated first, then the next-to-last LIFO layer, then the layer from the year before that, and so on until you reach total units sold.

To cost out ending inventory:

1,600	units in beginning inventory
−1,000	units liquidated
600	units in ending inventory

Total units in 20X4 ending inventory: 600

Year	Units sold	Unit cost	Total cost
20X1 LIFO layer	400	$2	$ 800
20X2 LIFO layer	+200*	3	+ 600
20X4 ending inventory.	600		$1,400

* 500 units in 20X2 LIFO layer – 300 units liquidated = 200 units remaining in 20X2 LIFO layer.

HaCo had to liquidate the entire 20X3 LIFO layer and a portion of the 20X2 LIFO layer to cost out its 20X4 COGS.

These computations illustrate why COGS is $34,400—and why ending inventory is $1,400. In reality, you would know ending inventory and would use the shorter cost of goods sold schedule to compute COGS. To compute:

$ 5,800	beginning inventory in 20X4
+30,000	net purchases
$35,800	available for sale
− 1,400	ending inventory
$34,400	cost of goods sold in 20X4

Sometimes a company's records show a total for ending inventory, but not the amount of each layer within ending inventory. If costing out goods sold requires you to liquidate layers, you will have to know the cost of each layer. The following problems and solutions demonstrate how to do this.

PROBLEM 8: XuCo begins operations in 20X6. XuCo's books show the following data (for purposes of illustration, all unit purchases within each year are at the same cost):

Ending inventory as of	Total units
December 31, 20X6	700
December 31, 20X7	1,100
December 31, 20X8	**2,100**
December 31, 20X9	1,500

In 20X6, XuCo paid $9 per unit; in 20X7, $13 per unit; in 20X8, $12 per unit; and in 20X9, $16 per unit. Compute the number of units in each layer of XuCo's 20X8 ending inventory and the cost of each layer.

SOLUTION 8: *To compute the number of units in each layer of XuCo's 20X8 ending inventory,* start with its first-year layer. In a company's first year, the LIFO layer is the same as its ending inventory.

The 20X6 LIFO layer is: 700 units x $9 per unit = $6,300 total cost.

To compute the 20X7 layer:

1,100	units in 20X7 ending inventory
− 700	units in 20X6 ending inventory (same as the LIFO layer in the first year)
400	units in 20X7 LIFO layer

Once you know the number of units in the layer, simply multiply this number by the cost per unit to find the cost of each layer.

The 20X7 LIFO layer is: 400 units x $13 per unit = $5,200 total cost.

To compute the 20X8 layer:

2,100	units in 20X8 ending inventory
−1,100	units in 20X7 ending inventory
1,000	units in 20X8 LIFO layer

The 20X8 LIFO layer is: 1,000 units x $12 per unit = $12,000 total cost.

PROBLEM 9: Using the information from Solution 8, compute the cost of XuCo's 20X8 ending inventory.

SOLUTION 9: Simply total the LIFO layers for each year computed in Solution 8.

To summarize the size and cost of each year's LIFO layer:

Year	Units in layer	Unit cost	Layer cost
20X6	700	$ 9	$ 6,300
20X7	400	13	5,200
20X8	1,000	12	+12,000
20X8 ending inventory			$23,500

PROBLEM 10: In 20X9, XuCo purchases 3,400 units at $16 each and sells 4,000 units. Using data from Problems 8 and 9, what is XuCo's 20X9 ending inventory?

SOLUTION 10: *To compute how many units were liquidated:*

4,000	units sold in 20X9
−3,400	units purchased in 20X9
600	units that must be liquidated from 20X9 beginning inventory

To compute how many units remain in ending inventory:

2,100	units in 20X9 beginning inventory
− 600	units liquidated
1,500	units in 20X9 ending inventory

To cost out ending inventory under LIFO, cost out units in the order they were purchased until you reach total units in ending inventory.

Total units in ending inventory: 1,500

	Year	Units in layer	Unit cost	Total cost
LIFO layer	20X6	700	$ 9	$ 6,300
LIFO layer	20X7	400	13	5,200
LIFO layer	20X8	+ 400*	12	+ 4,800
Ending inventory	20X9	1,500		$16,300

* 1,000 units originally in 20X8 layer – 600 units liquidated = 400 units remaining in 20X8 layer.

PROBLEM 11: Using the information from Problems 8 and 9, compute XuCo's 20X9 cost of goods sold.

SOLUTION 11: *To compute, use the cost of goods sold statement:*

$23,500	beginning inventory in 20X9
+54,400	net purchases (3,400 units x $16)
$77,900	available for sale
−16,300	ending inventory
$61,600	cost of goods sold in 20X9

PROBLEM 12: Prove the cost of goods sold computed in Problem 11.

SOLUTION 12: To compute the cost of goods sold under LIFO when a liquidation is required, liquidate the last layer (*last in*) first (*first out*), then the next-to-last LIFO layer and so on until total units sold are reached.

Total units sold in 20X9: 4,000

Year	Units sold	Unit cost	Total cost
20X9 purchases	3,400	$16	$54,400
20X8 LIFO layer	+ 600*	12	+ 7,200
Total	4,000	**COGS**	**$61,600**

* 4,000 units sold − 3,400 units purchased = 600 units liquidated from the 20X8 layer.

When LIFO Layers Contain Units of Multiple Costs

The preceding examples of LIFO layers have been based on a single cost for all units purchased during the year. But LIFO layers almost always include items purchased at different unit costs.

EXAMPLE 5: To illustrate, assume that ZiCo makes the following purchases in 20X7, its first year of business:

Purchase date	Units purchased	Unit cost	Total cost
May 9	400	$3	$ 1,200
August 27.	700	5	3,500
October 14	+ 900	6	+ 5,400
Total	2,000		$10,100

ZiCo's year-end physical count shows 500 units in ending inventory. Its ending inventory is computed as follows:

Total units in ending inventory: 500

Purchase date	Units	Unit cost	Total cost
May 9	400	$3	$1,200
August 27.	+100	5	+ 500
Ending inventory	500		$1,700

ZiCo's 20X7 LIFO layer and ending inventory is 500 units that cost $1,700.

But once a LIFO layer is created, you do not have to maintain different unit prices within the layer; instead, you can take a *weighted average* of the cost, using the following formula:

$$\frac{\$1,700 \text{ total cost of layer}}{500 \text{ units}} = \$3.40 \text{ weighted-average cost per unit}$$

This weighted average is applied only to units within a layer, never to units from different layers.

EXAMPLE 6: In 20X8, ZiCo shows the following data:

Units purchased	Unit cost	Total cost
1,800	$7	$12,600

During 20X8, ZiCo sells 2,100 units. At year end, a physical count shows 200 units in ending inventory.

1. What is ZiCo's 20X8 ending inventory? 2. What is its 20X8 cost of goods sold? 3. How do you prove ZiCo's 20X8 cost of goods sold?

1. To compute ZiCo's 20X8 ending inventory:

Total units in 20X8 ending inventory: 200

Year	Units sold	Unit cost	Total cost
20X7 LIFO layer	200*	$3.40**	$680

* 200 units were found in the physical count.
** This is the weighted average of units remaining in the 20X7 LIFO layer.

ZiCo's ending inventory for 20X8 is $680.

2. *To compute ZiCo's 20X8 cost of goods sold:* Use the cost of goods sold schedule:

$ 1,700	beginning inventory in 20X8 (same as 20X7 ending inventory)
+12,600	net purchases (1,800 units x $7)
$14,300	available for sale
− 680	ending inventory
$13,620	cost of goods sold in 20X8

3. *To prove ZiCo's 20X8 cost of goods sold:* First, compute how many units ZiCo must liquidate from its 20X8 beginning inventory to fulfill 20X8 sales:

To compute how many units must be liquidated:

2,100	units sold in 20X9
−1,800	units purchased in 20X9
300	units must be liquidated from 20X9 beginning inventory

Total units sold in 20X9: 2,100

Year	Units sold	Unit cost	Total cost
20X8 purchases	1,800	$7.00	$12,600
20X7 LIFO layer	+ 300*	3.40	+ 1,020
Total	2,100		$13,620

* 500 units originally in 20X7 layer − 200 units liquidated = 300 units remaining in 20X7 LIFO layer (the same number found in the 20X8 physical count).

Note: This method of costing out merchandise sold for the year can also be used when you need to know COGS before you know ending inventory.

PROBLEM 13: GuCo begins operations in 20X2 and shows the following data:

20X2	Units purchased	Unit cost	Total cost
March 19	600	$2	$1,200
November 6	+ 800	5	+4,000
Total	1,400		$5,200

GuCo's 20X2 physical count finds 900 units in ending inventory.

1. What is GuCo's 20X2 ending inventory? 2. What is the weighted-average cost per unit of its 20X2 LIFO layer?

SOLUTION 13:

1. *To compute GuCo's 20X2 ending inventory:*

Total units in 20X2 ending inventory: 900

Purchase date	Units sold	Unit cost	Total cost
March 19	600	$2	$1,200
November 6	+300	5	+1,500
Total ending inventory	900		$2,700

GuCo's 20X2 ending inventory is $2,700.

2. *To compute the weighted-average cost per unit of GuCo's 20X2 ending inventory:*

$$\frac{\$2,700 \text{ total cost of layer}}{900 \text{ units}} = \$3 \text{ weighted-avg cost per unit in the 20X2 LIFO layer}$$

PROBLEM 14: GuCo's 20X3 books show the following data:

Purchase date	Units purchased	Unit cost	Total cost
April 8	900	$6	$ 5,400
July 10	+1,200	9	+10,800
Total	2,100		$16,200

A physical count of GuCo's 20X3 ending inventory finds 400 units.

Using this data and the information in Problem 13, what is GuCo's 20X3 ending inventory?

SOLUTION 14: *To compute:*

Total units in 20X3 ending inventory: 400

Date	Units sold	Unit cost	Total cost
20X2 LIFO layer.	400	$3	$1,200

To cost out ending inventory, start with the earliest LIFO layer and continue costing out units in the order they were purchased. Because the 20X2 layer alone is beginning inventory for 20X3, all of the 400 units remaining in the 20X3 ending inventory are from the 20X2 layer.

PROBLEM 15: Using the information in Problems 13 and 14, compute GuCo's cost of goods sold in 20X3.

SOLUTION 15: *To compute GuCo's cost of goods sold:*

$ 2,700	beginning inventory in 20X3 (same as 20X2 ending inventory)
+16,200	net purchases
$18,900	available for sale
− 1,200	ending inventory
$17,700	cost of goods sold in 20X3

PROBLEM 16: Prove GuCo's 20X3 cost of goods sold.

SOLUTION 16: *To prove GuCo's 20X3 cost of goods sold,* first, compute how many units GuCo sold in 20X3:

900	units in 20X3 beginning inventory (same as 20X2 ending inventory)
+2,100	net purchases
3,000	units available for sale
− 400	ending inventory
2,600	units sold

Total units sold in 20X3: 2,600

Purchase date	Units sold	Unit cost	Total cost
July 10	1,200	$9	$10,800
April 8	900	6	5,400
20X2 LIFO layer	+ 500	3	+ 1,500
Total	2,600	**COGS**	**$17,700**

Note: This method of costing out merchandise sold for the year can also be used when you need to know COGS before you know ending inventory.

Income Tax Consequences

Under LIFO costing, when prices are rising, your company's expenses go up, its net income falls—and so do its taxes. The reason expenses go up is that sales are costed out using the most recent purchases; that is, those *last in*. If you select LIFO costing on the tax return, you must also use it for those financial statements prepared for outsiders (creditors, vendors, etc.).

QUIZ 1   INVENTORY COSTING USING THE LIFO METHOD

Problem I.

MeCo, which began operations in 20X1, uses the periodic inventory method and LIFO costing. It shows the following data:

Year	Units purchased	Unit cost	Units sold	Units in ending inventory
20X1	700	$12	500	200
20X2	2,200	18	1,600	

1. Cost out MeCo's 20X2 ending inventory by LIFO layer.

2. Find MeCo's 20X2 cost of goods sold.

3. Prove MeCo's 20X2 cost of goods sold.

Problem II.

RoCo begins operations in 20X3. It uses the periodic inventory method and LIFO costing.

Purchase date	Units purchased	Unit cost	Total cost
20X3			
March 23	400	$3	$1,200
July 21	900	4	3,600
November 20	+ 500	6	+3,000
Total	1,800		$7,800

At year-end 20X3, a physical count shows 1,000 units in ending inventory.

20X4			
February 4	700	$ 7	$ 4,900
June 29	1,100	10	11,000
October 11	+1,400	13	+18,200
Total	3,200		$34,100

At year-end 20X4, a physical count shows 1,900 units in ending inventory.

1. Cost out RoCo's ending inventory for 20X3.

2. Cost out RoCo's ending inventory for 20X4.

Problem III.

SuCo starts up in 20X7. It uses the periodic inventory method and LIFO costing.

Purchase date	Units purchased	Unit cost	Total cost
20X7			
January 3	300	$ 5	$ 1,500
April 2	800	7	5,600
August 9	900	8	7,200
November 29.	+ 700	11	+ 7,700
Total	2,700		$22,000
20X8			
January 10	600	$12	$ 7,200
April 8	1,000	13	13,000
May 9	1,500	16	24,000
November 1	+ 900	19	+17,100
Total	4,000		$61,300

SuCo sells 2,000 units of merchandise in 20X7 and 3,000 units in 20X8.

1. Using LIFO costing, compute SuCo's cost of goods sold in 20X7.

2. Using LIFO costing, compute SuCo's cost of goods sold in20X8.

Problem IV.

NoCo's merchandise purchases in 20X5 and 20X6 are as follows:

Purchase date	Units purchased	Unit cost	Total cost
20X5			
February 1	400	$12	$ 4,800
May 1	700	14	9,800
October 3	+1,100	20	+22,000
Total	2,200		$36,600
20X6			
January 3	700	$21	$14,700
June 1	1,300	23	29,900
Dececember 1	+1,000	25	+25,000
Total	3,000		$69,600

NoCo sells 1,200 units of merchandise in 20X5 and 3,300 units in 20X6. The company uses the periodic inventory method and LIFO costing.

1. Using LIFO costing, compute NoCo's cost of goods sold in 20X5.

2. Using LIFO costing, compute NoCo's cost of goods sold in 20X6.

Problem V.

1. After KaCo opens for business in 20X3, it shows the following data:

Year	Units purchased	Unit Cost	Units sold
20X3	2,500	$ 4	2,000
20X4	3,900	7	3,400
20X5	4,500	10	4,700

Compute KaCo's 20X5 cost of goods sold using LIFO costing. The company uses the periodic inventory method.

QUIZ 1   *Solutions and Explanations*

Problem I.

1. To compute MeCo's 20X2 ending inventory by layer, you must first compute the LIFO layer for 20X1:

To compute MeCo's 20X1 LIFO layer:

200* units in ending inventory x $12 per unit = $2,400 LIFO layer (same as ending inventory in the company's first year).

* 700 units purchased – 500 units sold.

To compute MeCo's 20X2 LIFO layer:

2,200	units purchased in 20X2
–1,600	units sold in 20X2
600	units in 20X2 LIFO layer

600 units in 20X2 LIFO layer x $18 per units = $10,800 cost of 20X2 LIFO layer.

To compute MeCo's 20X2 ending inventory:

$ 2,400	20X1 LIFO layer
+10,800	20X2 LIFO layer
$13,200	20X2 ending inventory

2. *To compute MeCo's 20X2 cost of goods sold:*

$ 2,400	20X2 beginning inventory
+39,600	20X2 net purchases (2,200 units x $18 per unit)
$42,000	available for sale
–13,200	20X2 ending inventory
$28,800	cost of goods sold

3. *To prove MeCo's 20X2 cost of goods sold:*

1,600 units sold x $18 per unit = $28,800 COGS.

Problem II.

1. *To compute RoCo's 20X3 ending inventory:* Start with the cost of units from the first purchase of the year and continue to cost out units in the order they were purchased until you reach total units in the 20X3 LIFO layer:

Total units in 20X3 ending inventory: 1,000

Purchase date	Units purchased	Unit cost	Total cost
March 23	400	$3	$1,200
July 21	+ 600	4	+2,400
Ending inventory* . . .	1,000		$3,600

* In a company's first year, ending inventory becomes the LIFO layer.

2. *To compute RoCo's 20X4 ending inventory:* First, compute the 20X4 LIFO layer:

1,900	units found in the 20X4 physical count
−1,000	units in 20X4 beginning inventory
900	units in the 20X4 LIFO layer.

Then, cost out the 20X4 LIFO layer:

Total units in the 20X4 LIFO layer: 900

Purchase date	Units purchased	Unit cost	Total cost
February 4	700	$ 7	$4,900
June 29.	+200	10	+2,000
Ending inventory	900		$6,900

Then, add the layers together to find 20X4 ending inventory:

$ 3,600	20X3 LIFO layer
+ 6,900	20X4 LIFO layer
$10,500	20X4 ending inventory

Problem III.

1. *To compute SuCo's 20X7 COGS:* Simply apply the computations used to prove cost of goods sold. Cost out units starting with the last purchase (last in) and work backward. Add the cost of units in the next-to-last purchase, the purchase before that and so on until you reach total units sold.

Total units sold in 20X7: 2,000

Purchase date	Units sold	Unit cost		Total cost
November 29	700	$11		$ 7,700
August 9	900	8		7,200
April 2	+ 400	7		+ 2,800
Total	2,000		COGS	$17,700

2. *To compute SuCo's 20X8 COGS:* For the 20X8 data, use the same approach given in #1 above:

Total units sold in 20X8: 3,000

Purchase date	Units sold	Unit cost		Total cost
November 1	900	$19		$17,100
May 9	1,500	16		24,000
April 8	+ 600	13		+ 7,800
Total	3,000		COGS	$48,900

Problem IV.

1. *To compute NoCo's 20X5 COGS:* Apply the computations used to prove cost of goods sold. That means costing out units in the last purchase (last in) and working backward by adding the cost of units in the next-to-last purchase, the purchase before that and so on until you reach total units sold.

Total units sold in 20X5: 1,200

Purchase date	Units sold	Unit cost		Total cost
October 3	1,100	$20		$22,000
May 1	+ 100	14		+ 1,400
Total	1,200		COGS	$23,400

2. *To compute NoCo's 20X6 COGS:* Because NoCo sold 3,300 units in 20X6 but purchased only 3,000, you will need to invade (cost out units from) beginning inventory . Thus, the first step is to compute 20X5 ending inventory:

To compute 20X5 ending inventory:

2,200	units purchased
−1,200	units sold
1,000	units in 20X5 ending inventory

To cost out 20X5 ending inventory, cost out units in the order in which they were purchased until you reach total units in ending inventory:

Total units in 20X5 ending inventory: 1,000

Purchase date	Units sold	Unit cost	Total cost
February 1	400	$12	$ 4,800
May 1	+ 600	14	+ 8,400
Ending inventory	1,000		$13,200

$$\frac{\$13{,}200 \text{ total cost of layer}}{1{,}000 \text{ units}} = \$13.20 \text{ weighted-average cost per unit}$$

Total units sold in 20X6: 3,300

Date	Units sold	Unit cost	Total cost
December 1	1,000	$25	$25,000
June 1	1,300	23	29,900
January 3	700	21	14,700
20X6 LIFO layer	+ 300	13.20	+ 3,960
Total	3,300	COGS	$73,560

Problem V.

1. Because KaCo sold 200 more units than it purchased in 20X5
(4,700 – 4,500), it will have to invade one or more LIFO layers in
beginning inventory to fulfill these sales. Thus, before you can
compute 20X5 cost of goods sold, you must compute the 20X4 LIFO
layer and possibly the 20X3 LIFO layer.

To compute the 20X4 LIFO layer:

3,900	units purchased
–3,400	units sold
500	units in 20X4 LIFO layer

500 units x $7 per unit = $3,500 cost of 20X4 LIFO layer.

The 20X4 LIFO layer contains the 200 units that were liquidated
so there is no need to compute the 20X3 LIFO layer. Cost out
units in the reverse order in which they were purchased:

Total units sold in 20X5: 4,700

Year	Units purchased	Unit cost		Total cost
20X5	4,500	$10		$45,000
20X4 LIFO layer.	+ 200	7		+ 1,400
Total	4,700		**COGS**	**$46,400**

QUIZ 2   INVENTORY COSTING USING THE LIFO METHOD

Problem I.

ReCo begins operations in 20X2 and uses the periodic inventory method and LIFO costing. ReCo's 20X2 merchandise purchases are as follows:

Purchase date	Units purchased	Unit cost	Total cost
March 25	600	$ 5	$ 3,000
June 3	900	6	5,400
August 17	1,100	8	8,800
December 2	+1,600	11	+17,600
Total	4,200		$34,800

ReCo's year-end physical count of inventory finds 1,000 units.

1. Compute ReCo's 20X2 ending inventory.

2. Compute ReCo's 20X2 cost of goods sold.

3. Prove ReCo's 20X2 cost of goods sold.

Problem II.

1. YiCo opens for business in 20X6 and and uses the periodic inventory method and LIFO costing. It purchases merchandise as follows:

Purchase date	Units purchased	Unit cost	Total cost	Units in ending inventory
20X6				
February 20	900	$ 7	$6,300	
August 12	700	8	5,600	
September 11	600	12	7,200	
December 31				1,100
20X7				
February 19	1,200	$17	$20,400	
August 10	2,200	30	66,000	
September 10	3,100	27	83,700	
December 31				1,800
20X8				
March 5.	1,000	$24	$ 24,000	
July 1.	2,500	28	70,000	
October 1.	4,400	33	145,200	
December 31				3,100

Compute YiCo's 20X8 ending inventory by computing the layers from earlier years.

Problem III.

1. BeCo's 20X4 beginning inventory is $13,700 and consists of the following layers:

Year	Units purchased	Unit cost	Total cost
20X1 LIFO layer.	500	$4	$ 2,000
20X2 LIFO layer.	900	7	6,300
20X3 LIFO layer	+ 600	9	+ 5,400
Total.	2,000		$13,700

During 20X4, BeCo buys 7,000 units at $11 each and sells 8,000 units. Compute BeCo's 20X4 cost of goods sold—then prove it. The company uses the periodic inventory method and LIFO costing.

Problem IV.

1. DoCo, a 20X8 start-up that uses the periodic method and LIFO costing, makes the following purchases in 20X8:

Purchase date	Units purchased	Unit cost	Total cost
January 17	900	$15	$ 13,500
March 9	2,200	14	30,800
May 5	3,400	17	57,800
July 5	1,100	22	24,200
September 10	4,400	20	88,000
November 30	+ 800	26	+ 20,800
Total.	12,800		$235,100

DoCo's 20X8 year-end physical count finds 5,000 units, and its 20X9 physical count finds 4,200 units. Compute DoCo's 20X9 ending inventory. The company uses the periodic inventory method and LIFO costing.

Problem V.

PaCo starts up in 20X6 and uses the periodic inventory method and LIFO costing. During its first four years of operations, PaCo's merchandise purchases and sales are as follows:

Year	Units purchased	Unit Cost	Unit sold
20X6	2,800	$14	2,100
20X7	5,800	16	5,500
20X8	6,400	22	6,800
20X9	7,700	25	7,500

1. Compute PaCo's 20X8 ending inventory.

2. Compute PaCo's 20X9 ending inventory.

QUIZ 2   Solutions and Explanations

Problem I.

1. *To cost out ReCo's 20X2 ending inventory:* Start with the cost of units purchased first, and continue to cost out units in the order in which they were purchased until you reach total units in ending inventory.

    Total units in 20X2 ending inventory: 1,000

Purchase date	Units	Unit cost	Total cost
March 25	600	$5	$3,000
June 3	+ 400	6	+2,400
Ending inventory	1,000		$5,400

2. *To compute ReCo's 20X2 cost of goods sold:*

$ 0	beginning inventory in 20X2
+34,800	net purchases
$34,800	available for sale
– 5,400	ending inventory
$29,400	20X2 COGS

3. *To prove ReCo's 20X2 cost of goods sold:* First, determine the number of units sold:

4,200	units purchased
–1,000	units in year-end physical count
3,200	units sold

    Then, compute the cost of units in the last purchase of the year and work backward, costing out the units in the next-to-last purchase, the purchase before that and so on until total units sold are reached.

    Total units sold in 20X2: 3,200

Purchase date	Units sold	Unit cost	Total cost
December 2.	1,600	$11	$17,600
August 17.	1,100	8	8,800
June 3	+ 500	6	+ 3,000
Total	3,200	COGS	$29,400

Problem II.

1. *To compute YiCo's 20X8 ending inventory:* Compute its 20X8 beginning inventory. That requires computing the LIFO layers for 20X6 and 20X7, the two layers that will make up 20X8 beginning inventory.

To compute YiCo's 20X6 LIFO layer: Compute ending inventory, the same as the LIFO layer in the company's first year. Start with the cost of units purchased first and continue to cost out units in the order in which they were purchased until you reach total units in ending inventory.

Total units in 20X6 ending inventory: 1,100

Purchase date	Units sold	Unit cost	Total cost
February 20	900	$7	$6,300
August 12	+ 200	8	+1,600
Total	1,100		$7,900

The 20X6 LIFO layer is 1,100 units, costed out at $7,900.

To compute the 20X7 LIFO layer: First, compute the number of units in the layer:

1,800	units in ending inventory
−1,100	units in beginning inventory
700	units in 20X7 LIFO layer

Then, compute the LIFO layer by costing out the units purchased first and continuing to cost out the units in the order in which they were purchased until you reach total units in the LIFO layer. For 20X7, the entire layer can be taken from the first purchase of the year:

Total units in 20X7 LIFO layer: 700

Purchase date	Units sold	Unit cost	Total cost
February 19	700	$17	$11,900

The 20X7 LIFO layer is 700 units costed out at $11,900.

To compute the 20X8 LIFO layer: First, compute the number of units in the layer:

3,100	units in ending inventory
−1,800*	units in beginning inventory
1,300	units in 20X8 LIFO layer

* 1,100	units in 20X6 LIFO layer
+ 700	units in 20X7 LIFO layer
1,800	units in 20X8 beginning inventory

Then, compute the 20X8 LIFO layer by costing out the units in the order in which they were purchased:

Total units in 20X8 LIFO layer: 1,300

Purchase date	Units sold	Unit cost	Total cost
March 5.	1,000	$24	$24,000
July 1.	+ 300	28	+ 8,400
Total	1,300		$32,400

The 20X8 LIFO layer is 1,300 units costed out at $32,400.

Then compute ending inventory by adding together 20X6, 20X7 and 20X8 layers:

$ 7,900	20X6 LIFO layer of	1,100 units	
11,900	20X7 LIFO layer of	700 units	
+32,400	20X8 LIFO layer of	+1,300 units	
$52,200		3,100	

YiCo's 20X8 ending inventory is $52,200.

Problem III.

1. There are two ways to find BeCo's COGS for 20X4.

The first way to compute BeCo's 20X4 COGS: Use the cost of goods sold schedule. To find the only cost missing, 20X4 ending inventory, compute the number of units in ending inventory. In 20X4, BeCo sold 8,000 units but bought only 7,000, so that 1,000 units had to be liquidated from beginning inventory:

2,000	units in beginning inventory (total of previous years' layers)
−1,000	units liquidated during the year
1,000	units in ending inventory

To compute 20X4 ending inventory, cost out the units in the earliest purchase—in this case begin with the earliest layer—and continue costing out units in the order in which they were purchased until you reach total units in ending inventory:

Total units in 20X4 ending inventory: 1,000

Year	Units purchased	Unit cost	Total cost
20X1 base layer	500	$4	$2,000
20X2 LIFO layer	+ 500	7	+3,500
Ending inventory	1,000		$5,500

Now you can use the cost of goods sold schedule to compute COGS:

$13,700*	beginning inventory in 20X4
+77,000**	net purchases
$90,700	available for sale
− 5,500	ending inventory
$85,200	20X4 COGS

* Beginning inventory is the sum of all the previous years' LIFO layers.
** 7,000 units x $11 per unit = $77,000.

The second way to compute BeCo's 20X4 COGS: Use the computation normally reserved for proving cost of goods sold. That is, compute the cost of units in the last purchase of the year and work backward, costing out the units in the next-to-last purchase, the purchase before that and so on. If, before reaching total units sold, you run out of purchases for the year, cost out the units starting with last year's LIFO layer, then the layer before that and so on until you reach total units sold:

Total units sold in 20X4: 8,000

Year	Units sold	Unit cost	Total cost
20X4 purchases	7,000	$11	$77,000
20X3 LIFO layer	600	9	5,400
20X2 LIFO layer	+ 400	7	+ 2,800
Total	8,000	**COGS**	**$85,200**

Problem IV.

1. DoCo's 20X9 ending inventory will include units from the 20X8 LIFO layer, so you must compute the 20X8 layer by costing out units in the order they were purchased until you reach total units in ending inventory:

Total units in 20X8 ending inventory: 5,000

Purchase date	Units purchased	Unit cost	Total cost
January 17	900	$15	$13,500
March 9.	2,200	14	30,800
May 5.	+1,900	17	+32,300
Total	5,000		$76,600

Next, compute the weighted-average cost per unit of the 20X8 LIFO layer:

$$\frac{\$76,600 \text{ total cost of layer}}{5,000 \text{ units}} = \$15.32 \text{ weighted-average cost per unit}$$

In 20X9, DoCo liquidated 800 units from the LIFO layer of 5,000, leaving 4,200 units in the layer.

4,200 units remaining in the 20X8 LIFO layer x $15.32 per unit = $64,344 ending inventory in 20X9.

Problem V.

1. To find PaCo's 20X8 ending inventory, you must find its 20X8 beginning inventory. That requires computing the LIFO layers for the previous years.

To compute the 20X6 LIFO layer:

2,800	units purchased
–2,100	units sold
700	units in 20X6 LIFO layer

700 units x $14 per unit = $9,800 cost of PaCo's 20X6 LIFO layer.

To compute the 20X7 LIFO layer:

5,800	units purchased
–5,500	units sold
300	units in 20X7 LIFO layer

300 units x $16 per unit = $4,800 cost of PaCo's 20X7 LIFO layer.

To compute 20X8 ending inventory: Because PaCo sold more units than it bought in 20X8, to cost out the units sold it had to invade beginning inventory and liquidate one or more LIFO layers.

To compute how many units PaCo had to liquidate in 20X8:

6,800	units sold
–6,400	units purchased
400	units liquidated in 20X8

Total units liquidated in 20X8: 400

Year	Units sold	Unit cost	Total cost
20X7 LIFO layer	300	$16	$4,800
20X6 LIFO layer	+100	14	+1,400
Total liquidation	400		$6,200

Note: All of the 20X7 LIFO layer and a portion of the 20X6 LIFO layer have now been liquidated.

To compute how many units are in 20X8 ending inventory:

700	units in 20X6 LIFO layer
+ 300	units in 20X7 LIFO layer
1,000	units in 20X8 beginning inventory
– 400	units liquidated in 20X8
600*	units in 20X8 ending inventory

* These units are from the 20X6 LIFO layer because the 20X7 LIFO layer was liquidated to cost out goods sold in 20X8.

To compute 20X8 ending inventory, cost out units in the order they were purchased, starting with the first LIFO layer. For PaCo, all the units currently in ending inventory are from the 20X6 LIFO layer:

Total units in 20X8 ending inventory: 600

Date	Units purchased	Unit cost	Total cost
20X6 LIFO layer.	600*	$14	$8,400

* 700 units originally in the 20X6 LIFO layer – 100 units liquidated to cost out goods sold in 20X8 = 600 units remaining in the 20X6 LIFO layer.

PaCo's 20X8 ending inventory is $8,400.

2. To compute 20X9 ending inventory, you must first compute the 20X9 LIFO layer.

To compute the 20X9 LIFO layer:

7,700	units purchased
–7,500	units sold
200*	units in 20X9 LIFO layer

* This computation was explained on page 137.

200 units x $25 per units = $5,000 cost of 20X9 LIFO layer.

To compute 20X9 ending inventory:

Year	Units purchased	Unit cost	Total cost
20X6 LIFO layer	600	$14	$ 8,400
20X9 LIFO layer	+200	25	+ 5,000
Ending inventory	800		$13,400

Important: 20X9 ending inventory contains only the 20X6 LIFO layer and the 20X9 LIFO layer; the 20X7 layer was liquidated to cost out sales in 20X8 when PaCo sold more units than it purchased. Also, because PaCo sold more units than it purchased in 20X8, no 20X8 layer was created.

INVENTORY COSTING USING THE LOWER OF COST OR MARKET RULE

Introduction

A company may choose to cost out its inventory using FIFO, LIFO, or weighted-average costing. However, sometimes the value of merchandise inventory declines below the original cost. When this occurs, generally accepted accounting principles (GAAP) require the company to recognize and report the loss in the period of decline, as follows:

- If the current market value is lower than the original cost, then the inventory is shown on the balance sheet at the current market value.

- If the original cost is lower than the current market value, then the inventory is shown on the balance sheet at the original cost.

At the end of each period, a company must apply this *lower of cost or market* (LCM) rule, or measurement, to determine the value of its inventory under GAAP.

Cost and Market Defined

Cost is the amount at which the particular items are shown in the Inventory account.

Market (the shorthand term for market value) is the current replacement cost, generally what the company would currently have to pay to buy the inventory. However, you can use the current replacement cost for market only if this cost does not exceed the *ceiling* and is not lower than the *floor*.

The *ceiling*, or upper limit, is the *net realizable value* (NRV). It is computed as follows:

Estimated selling price
    − Disposal costs (sales costs)
Ceiling (net realizable value)

If the replacement cost exceeds the ceiling, then the ceiling becomes market.

For example, LuCo's estimated selling price is $40 per unit, which includes $9 per unit sales (disposal) costs. What is LuCo's per unit ceiling (NRV)?

$40	estimated selling price per unit
– 9	disposal costs per unit
$31	ceiling (NRV) per unit

If LuCo's replacement cost is higher than the ceiling of $31 per unit, the $31 ceiling becomes market.

The *floor*, or lower limit, is computed as follows:

Ceiling (NRV)
– Estimated normal mark-up
Floor

Assume that LuCo's estimated normal mark-up is $6 per unit. LuCo computes the floor as follows:

$31	ceiling (NRV) (computed above) per unit
– 6	estimated normal mark-up per unit
$25	floor per unit

If the replacement cost is below $25, then the $25 floor becomes market.

How to Determine Market

To determine market:

Step 1: Find the replacement cost.

Step 2: Compute the ceiling.

Step 3: Compute the floor.

Step 4: If the replacement cost is higher than the ceiling, you must use the ceiling for market. If the replacement cost is lower than the floor, you must use the floor for market. If the replacement cost does not exceed the ceiling and is not lower than the floor, you must use the replacement cost for market value.

Using Lower of Cost or Market to Compute Ending Inventory

After you have determined market, compare it to the carrying value (the amount shown for the particular item(s) in the Inventory account). The lower amount (that is, the lower of cost or market) is the amount that will go on the balance sheet as ending inventory.

LCM Illustrated

ZiCo's inventory consists of four items that cost $120 each:

Item	Original cost
A	$120
B	120
C	120
D	120

Step 1: ZiCo determines the following replacement cost for each item:

Item	Replacement cost
A	$106
B	122
C	116
D	114

Step 2: ZiCo computes the ceiling for each product (selling price and disposal cost are given) as follows:

	Item A	Item B	Item C	Item D
Selling price (given)	$118	$136	$120	$132
– Disposal cost	– 6	– 6	– 6	– 6
Ceiling (NRV)	**$112**	**$130**	**$114**	**$126**

Step 3: ZiCo computes the floor for each product (normal mark-up per item is given):

	Item A	Item B	Item C	Item D
Ceiling (NRV)	$112	$130	$114	$126
– Normal mark-up	– 8	– 8	– 8	– 8
Floor	**$104**	**$122**	**$106**	**$118**

Step 4: ZiCo determines market for each item. When the replacement cost is higher than the ceiling, ZiCo must use the ceiling for market. When the replacement cost is lower than the floor, ZiCo must use the floor for market. When the replacement cost does not the exceed ceiling or fall below the floor, ZiCo must use the replacement cost as the market. ZiCo determines LCM for each item as follows:

Item	Cost*	Replacement cost	Ceiling (NRV)	Floor	Market		Item at LCM	
A	$120	$106	$112	$104	$106	(r)	$106	(m)
B	120	122	130	122	122	(r)	120	(c)
C	120	116	114	106	114	(c)	114	(m)
D	120	114	126	118	118	(f)	118	(m)

* Given.

c = ceiling
f = floor
r = replacement cost

c = cost
m = market

Here is how ZiCo first determined market, then the lower of cost or market for each item.

Item A: The $106 replacement cost was lower than the $112 ceiling and higher than the $104 floor; therefore, the $106 replacement cost became market. The $106 market was lower than the $120 original cost, so for Item A, ZiCo used market.

Item B: The $122 replacement cost was lower than the $130 ceiling and the same as the $122 floor; therefore, the $122 replacement cost became market. The $120 original cost was lower than the $122 market, so for Item B, ZiCo used cost.

Item C: The $116 replacement cost was higher than the $114 ceiling, so the $114 ceiling became market. The $114 market was lower than the $120 original cost, so for Item C, ZiCo used market.

Item D: The $114 replacement cost was lower than the $118 floor, so the $118 floor became market. The $118 market was lower than the $120 original cost, so for Item D, ZiCo used market.

Three Ways to Apply LCM

When ending inventory includes a variety of products, you can apply LCM three different ways.

1. Apply LCM item by item. Apply LCM to each item, then total the LCM for all items to arrive at ending inventory.

2. Apply LCM group by group (also referred to as "by classification" or "by class"). A *group* may be whatever the company decides, such as a department (one group for sporting goods, another for menswear); product (one group for sweaters, another for jackets); price (one group for items under $10, another for items between $11 and $50, and so on); location (one group for items at the Chicago store, another for items at the New York store); or some other classification.

3. Apply LCM to total inventory. Add up the original cost of all items in ending inventory, then determine and add up market for all items in ending inventory. The lower amount becomes ending inventory.

Applying LCM item by item always results in the lowest amount for ending inventory on the balance sheet. A company may select any of the three methods, but it must continue to use that method year after year.

Illustrations of the Three Ways to Apply LCM

At the end of BiCo's first year of business, management must decide whether it wants to compute ending inventory at LCM item by item, group by group, or total inventory. BiCo's accounting department assembles the following data (market has been determined):

Item	Total units	Unit at cost	Unit at market
A1	100	$20	$17
A2	300	33	35
A3	600	13	12
B1	500	44	40
B2	200	51	55
C1	700	8	5
C2	900	6	11

1. Applying LCM item by item

1. For each item, determine market, then compare market to cost and choose the lower of cost or market.

2. *Multiply:* Number of units of item x LCM per unit = LCM for the item.

3. *Add*: LCM amount for all items to yield the amount for ending inventory.

For BiCo, these totals are as follows:

Item	Unit at cost	Unit at market	Unit at LCM		Total units		Item at LCM
A1	$20	$17	$17 (m)	x	100	=	$ 1,700 (m)
A2	33	35	33 (c)	x	300	=	9,900 (c)
A3	13	12	12 (m)	x	600	=	7,200 (m)
B1	44	40	40 (m)	x	500	=	20,000 (m)
B2	51	55	51 (c)	x	200	=	10,200 (c)
C1	8	5	5 (m)	x	700	=	3,500 (m)
C2	6	11	6 (c)	x	900	=	+ 5,400 (c)
			Ending inventory applying LCM item by item				**$57,900**

2. Applying LCM group by group (or by class)

1. *Multiply*: Number of units of item x cost per unit = total cost of item.

2. *Add*: Cost of all items in group to yield cost of group.

3. Determine market for each item, then *multiply*: Number of units of item x market per unit = total market for item.

4. *Add*: Market for all items in group to yield market for the group.

5. Compare the cost of each group to market for each group and select the lower amount. Add up the lower amount for all groups to arrive at ending inventory.

For BiCo these totals are as follows:

Group	Item	Total units		Unit at cost		Item at cost	Group at cost	Unit at market		Item at market	Group at market	Group at LCM	
Group A	...A1	100	x	$20	=	$ 2,000		$17	=	$ 1,700			
	...A2	300	x	33	=	9,900		35	=	10,500			
	...A3	600	x	13	=	+ 7,800		12	=	+ 7,200			
Total A							$19,700				$19,400	$19,400	(m)
Group B	...B1	500	x	44	=	22,000		40	=	20,000			
	...B2	200	x	51	=	+10,200		55	=	+11,000			
Total B							$32,200				$31,000	$31,000	(m)
Group C	...C1	700	x	8	=	5,600		5	=	3,500			
	...C2	900	x	6	=	+ 5,400		11	=	+ 9,900			
Total C							$11,000				$13,400	+$11,000	(c)

Ending inventory applying LCM group by group $61,400

3. Applying LCM to total inventory

1. *Multiply*: Number of units of item x cost per unit = total cost of item.

2. *Add*: The cost of all items in inventory to yield ending inventory at cost.

3. Determine market for each item, then *multiply*: Number of units of item x market per unit = total of each item at market.

4. *Add*: Market for all items in inventory to yield ending inventory at market.

5. Use the lower of cost (2) or market (4) for ending inventory.

For BiCo, applying LCM to total inventory is done as follows:

Item	Total units		Unit at cost		Item at cost	Unit at market		Item at market
A1	100	x	$20	=	$ 2,000	$17	=	$ 1,700
A2	300	x	33	=	9,900	35	=	10,500
A3	600	x	13	=	7,800	12	=	7,200
B1	500	x	44	=	22,000	40	=	20,000
B2	200	x	51	=	10,200	55	=	11,000
C1	700	x	8	=	5,600	5	=	3,500
C2	900	x	6	=	+ 5,400	11	=	+ 9,900
			Applying LCM to total inventory at cost		**$62,900**	Applying LCM to total inventory at market		**$63,800**

Applying LCM to total inventory, BiCo finds that the cost of $62,900 is lower than the market of $63,800; therefore, BiCo uses the cost for ending inventory.

In practice, BiCo's accounting department would put the results of the three LCM applications (by item, by group, and by total inventory) on a single chart so that management could make the final decision on which application of LCM it wanted to use. Once management makes its selection, it must apply it consistently in subsequent years.

Summary of the three LCM applications for BiCo

Item	Total units	1. By item	2. By group	3. By total inventory
A1	100	$ 1,700 (market)		
A2	300	9,900 (cost)		
A3	600	7,200 (market)		
Total A			$19,400 (market)	
B1	500	20,000 (market)		
B2	200	10,200 (cost)		
Total B			31,000 (market)	
C1	700	3,500 (market)		
C2	900	+ 5,400 (cost)		
Total C			+11,000 (cost)	
		$57,900	**$61,400**	**$62,900**

PROBLEM 1: CaCo shows the following data (market has been determined):

Item	Total units	Unit at cost	Unit at market
Gx	100	$24	$27
Gy	50	33	31
Lm	60	22	24
Lp	80	15	11
Lr	20	51	55
Dh	70	18	25
Dz	40	36	27

What is CaCo's ending inventory applying LCM item by item?

SOLUTION 1:

Item	Total units	Unit at LCM	Total item at LCM
Gx	100	$24 (c)	$2,400 (c)
Gy	50	31 (m)	1,550 (m)
Lm	60	22 (c)	1,320 (c)
Lp	80	11 (m)	880 (m)
Lr	20	51 (c)	1,020 (c)
Dh	70	18 (c)	1,260 (c)
Dz	40	27 (m)	+1,080 (m)
Ending inventory applying LCM by item			**$9,510**

PROBLEM 2: Using the data from Problem 1, compute CaCo's ending inventory applying LCM to total inventory.

SOLUTION 2:

Item	Total units	Unit at cost	Item at cost	Unit at market	Item at market
Gx	100	$24	$ 2,400	$27	$ 2,700
Gy	50	33	1,650	31	1,550
Lm	60	22	1,320	24	1,440
Lp	80	15	1,200	11	880
Lr	20	51	1,020	55	1,100
Dh	70	18	1,260	25	1,750
Dz	40	36	+ 1,440	27	+ 1,080
		Ending inventory applying LCM at cost	**$10,290**	**Ending inventory applying LCM at market**	**$10,500**

When LCM is applied to total inventory, CaCo's ending inventory is $10,290 (cost).

PROBLEM 3: Using the data from Problem 2, calculate CaCo's ending inventory applying LCM by class. Class G is Gx and Gy, Class L is Lm, Lp and Lr; and Class D is Dh and Dz.

SOLUTION 3:

Class/item	Total units	Unit at cost	Item at cost	Class at cost	Unit at market	Item at market	Class at market	LCM
Class G								
Gx	100	$24	$2,400		$27	$2,700		
Gy	50	33	+1,650		31	+1,550		
Total G				$ 4,050			$ 4,250	$ 4,050 (c)
Class L								
Lm.	60	22	1,320		24	1,440		
Lp	80	15	1,200		11	880		
Lr.	20	51	+1,020		55	+1,100		
Total L				$ 3,540			$ 3,420	$ 3,420 (m)
Class D								
Dh	70	18	1,260		25	1,750		
Dz	40	36	+1,440		27	+ 1,080		
Total D				+$ 2,700			+$ 2,830	+$ 2,700 (c)
				$10,290			**$10,500**	**$10,170**

When LCM is applied by class, ending inventory is $10,170.

When There Is a *Temporary* Decline in the Value of Inventory

Inventory is often worth more in season and less out of season. For example, skis are worth more in the winter and less in the summer, and swimwear is worth more in the summer and less in the winter. To assure that temporary declines do not affect the financial statements, a temporary decline is ignored, and inventory is recorded at the cost.

When There Is a *Permanent* Decline in the Value of Inventory

Sometimes events permanently reduce the value of inventory. For example, a competitor introduces a new technology, cuts its list price, or the market changes in some way that makes current inventory worth less.

When applying LCM results in cost being higher than market, the difference is treated as a loss.

There are two ways to record the loss depending on the amount:

- If the amount of the loss is not significant enough to warrant disclosure on the income statement, it is debited to Cost of Goods Sold, as follows:

Cost of Goods Sold   xxxx
    Inventory*   xxxx
* Instead of Inventory, the account Allowance to Reduce Inventory to Market may be used. This is a contra account (subtracted from Inventory) on the balance sheet.

- If the loss is significant enough and meets certain conditions, it will be reported on the income statement as a deduction against ordinary income. The conditions that must be met are as follows:

1. It is *probable* that the price will remain lower.
2. The loss can by *reasonably* estimated.
3. The estimated loss is *material* (significant).

A loss that is significant and meets these conditions is recorded as follows:

Loss on Inventory Writedown to Market[1]   xxxx
    Inventory[2]   xxxx
[1] This account is created to hold the loss.

[2] Instead of Inventory, the account Allowance to Reduce Inventory to Market may be used, as explained in the previous journal entry on this page.

When There Is a Recovery in the Value of Inventory

If, after recording a loss, the inventory recovers some of its value, the lower of cost or market rule does not permit the company to recognize this recovery unless the allowance account is used (see the footnote to the first journal entry at the top of this page). If the allowance account is used, a loss recovery may be recognized up to the amount of the previous write-down of inventory.

PROBLEM 4: LaCo, a distributor of crystal wine glasses, has $300,000 in inventory. In November, 20X6, a competitor offers chip-proof glasses. On December 31, when LaCo prepares its balance sheet, it decides that its inventory's selling price has been permanently lowered by the chip-proof product and that it could replace its current nonchip-proof inventory at a lower price. Applying LCM, LaCo determines the loss at $1,200. In February, 20X7, LaCo realizes the chip-proof glasses have had little effect on its inventory, so management decides to revalue the inventory upward by $2,000. What entries does LaCo make to record these events?

SOLUTION 4: LaCo decides that the decline is not substantial enough to warrant disclosure on its income statement, so it records the decline in Cost of Goods Sold:

<u>December 31, 20X6</u>

Cost of Goods Sold	1,200	
Inventory*		1,200

To record decline in value of inventory

* The account, Allowance to Reduce Inventory to Market, may also be used.

Once LaCo has reduced the value of its inventory, the LCM rule does not permit LaCo to recognize the recovery if the credit in the entry above was made to Inventory. If the credit was made to Allowance to Reduce Inventory to Market, however, a recovery may be recorded up to the amount of the previous write-down, as follows:

Allowance to Reduce Inventory to Market	1,200	
Loss Recovery Due to Reduction		
of Inventory to Market		1,200

To record recovery in inventory value written down under LCM

PROBLEM 5: In August, 20X7, LaCo (from Problem 4) decides that a widely publicized warning about the lead content of crystal glasses will permanently lower the anticipated selling price of its inventory and that it would be able to replace its current inventory for less than the original cost. On December 31, 20X7, when LaCo prepares its financial statements, it applies LCM and computes a loss of $30,000. On March 31, 20X8, when LaCo is preparing interim financial statements for the first quarter, it realizes that the bad publicity has had little effect on sales and that the loss will be only $25,000. What entries does LaCo make to record these events?

SOLUTION 5: LaCo determines that the $30,000 loss in the value of its inventory is substantial enough to warrant disclosure on its income statement where it will be treated as a deduction against ordinary income. Thus, LaCo records the decline in Loss on Inventory Writedown to Market, as follows:

<u>December 31, 20X7</u>

Loss on Inventory Writedown to Market	30,000	
Inventory*		30,000

* The account, Allowance to Reduce Inventory to Market, may also be used.

The $5,000 gain ($30,000 anticipated loss – $25,000 actual loss) is not recognized if the credit in the entry above was made to Inventory. If, however, the credit was made to Allowance to Reduce Inventory to Market, the recovery may be recorded up to the amount of the previous write-down, as follows:

<u>March 31, 20X8</u>

Allowance to Reduce Inventory to Market	5,000	
Loss Recovery Due to Reduction		
of Inventory to Market		5,000

*   To record recovery in inventory value written down under LCM*

Loss on Purchase Commitment

A purchase commitment is a contract that obligates the buyer to purchase merchandise at a specified price on a specified date. When the buyer signs a purchase commitment, it does not record an entry in the ledger accounts because no transaction has taken place (although it might record a memo that the contract was signed).

- If, on the delivery date, the market price is higher than the commitment price, the increase is ignored because the buyer will pay the lower price set in the purchase commitment.

- If, on the delivery date, the market price is lower than the commitment price, the buyer records the merchandise at the lower delivery date price, pays the higher purchase commitment amount and records a loss for the difference.

Sometimes the buyer signs a purchase agreement just before the end of the year or quarter and must prepare financial statements before the delivery date. If this occurs, the buyer checks the market price on the balance sheet date. If the price is lower and the contract is noncancelable, the buyer records the loss as follows:

Estimated Loss on Purchase Commitment	xxxx	
Estimated Liability on Purchase Commitment*		xxxx

* This account is shown as a liability on the Balance Sheet.

- **If the market price recovers after the loss is recognized but before the delivery date,** then on the delivery date the purchase is recorded at the higher amount—but never higher than the price actually paid. The amount of the recovery is recognized and recorded in Recovery of Loss on Purchase Commitment:

Estimated Liability on Purchase Commitment   xxxx
    Recovery of Loss on Purchase Commitment   xxxx

- **If the market price declines further between the date that the loss is recognized and the delivery date,** then on the delivery date the additional loss is recognized.

PROBLEM 6: SeCo uses the perpetual method.

1. On December 11, 20X1, SeCo signs a purchase commitment to buy merchandise on January 22, 20X2 for $40,000.

2. On December 31, 20X1, when SeCo prepares its balance sheet, the market price of the merchandise is $37,000.

3. On January 22, 20X2, SeCo takes delivery of the goods.

What entries must SeCo record on the delivery date if the market price is $36,000 and SeCo pays $40,000 cash?

SOLUTION 6: SeCo records the following entries:

December 11, 20X1
There is no entry when a company signs a purchase commitment.

December 31, 20X1

Estimated Loss on Purchase Commitment   3,000*
    Estimated Liability on Purchase Commitment   3,000

* $40,000 commitment price – $37,000 year-end market price = $3,000 loss on market decline.

January 22, 20X2
Inventory   36,000
Estimated Liability on
   Purchase Commitment   3,000   **(original decline in 20X1)**
Loss on Purchase
   Commitment   1,000*   **(additional decline in 20X2)**
    Cash   40,000

* $37,000 year-end market price – $36,000 delivery date market price = $1,000 *additional* loss on market decline in 20X2.

Explanation of the January 22 entry: When the transaction is booked on the delivery date, the purchase is recorded at the current market price of $36,000 (which accounts for the additional $1,000 loss). When SeCo pays the liability, it closes out the Estimated Liability on Purchase Commitment.

PROBLEM 7: On November 14, 20X8, TiCo signs a contract commitment to purchase merchandise on account for $19,000 for delivery in February, 20X9. On the balance sheet date, December 31, 20X8, the market price has declined to $16,200. On the delivery date, February 28, 20X9, the market price has recovered to $16,800. What entries does TiCo use to record these events?

SOLUTION 7: TiCo records the following entries:

November 14, 20X8
There is no entry when a company signs a purchase commitment.

December 31, 20X8

Estimated Loss on Purchase Commitment	2,800*	
Estimated Liability on Purchase Commitment		2,800

* $19,000 commitment price – $16,200 market price on balance sheet date = $2,800 loss on market decline.

February 28, 20X9

Inventory	16,800	
Estimated Liability on Purchase Commitment	2,800	
Recovery of Loss on Purchase Commitment		600*
Cash		19,000

* $16,800 delivery date market price – $16,200 market price on balance sheet date = $600 recovery of market decline.

QUIZ 1 INVENTORY COSTING USING THE LOWER OF COST OR MARKET RULE

Problem I.

On December 31, 20X5, PoCo shows the following data for ending inventory:

Item	Cost*	Replacement cost	Selling price*	Disposal cost	Normal mark-up
A	$64	$ 63	$ 68	$ 7	$10
B	82	80	94	9	12
C	38	37	63	8	15
D	95	109	125	18	22
E	47	39	65	10	15

* Given.

1. Determine market for each item. Hint: To find market, you must first determine the ceiling and the floor.

2. Compute ending inventory applying LCM item by item.

Problem II.

LiCo's inventory on December 31, 20X2, consists of four different chairs. The quantities, cost per unit, and market (market has been determined) per unit are as follows:

Item	Total units	Unit at cost	Unit at market
Wooden chairs...... 100		$72	$67
Metal chairs 300		33	35
Plastic chairs....... 600		13	19
Beach chairs 500		11	12

Calculate LiCo's ending inventory applying LCM item by item.

Problem III.

DiCo's inventory on December 31, 20X9 consists of the following:

Item	Total units	Unit at cost	Unit at market
AM	400	$20	$22
AM/FM.	600	53	49
AM with alarm	500	36	34
AM/FM with alarm. .	900	77	78

Calculate DiCo's ending inventory applying LCM to total inventory.

Problem IV.

As of December 31, 20X6, HuCo had an inventory consisting of seven items divided into three classes, as follows:

Product	Total units	Unit at cost	Unit at market
Residential			
Sofas	10	$280	$250
Armchairs	30	140	160
Office			
Desks	40	190	170
Bookcases	50	110	120
Swivel chairs.	30	220	205
Commercial			
Display cases.	70	400	410
Chairs	80	90	70

Calculate HuCo's inventory on December 31, 20X6, based on applying the lower of cost or market rule by class.

Problem V.

On December 4, 20X5, CuCo signs a purchase commitment to buy 1,000 ounces of Rutex at $19 an ounce for delivery in February, 20X6. Terms are net 30. On December 31, 20X5, when CuCo prepares its balance sheet, the market price of Rutex is $16 an ounce. On February 23, 20X6, the delivery date, the market price has recovered to $18 an ounce. CuCo pays the invoice on March 22, 20X6. Prepare CuCo's entries for these events.

QUIZ 1 Solutions and Explanations

Problem I.

1. To compute market, you must first compute the ceiling and the floor:

	Item A	Item B	Item C	Item D	Item E
Selling price (given)	$68	$94	$63	$125	$65
– Disposal cost	– 7	– 9	– 8	– 18	–10
Ceiling (NRV)	**$61**	**$85**	**$55**	**$107**	**$55**

	Item A	Item B	Item C	Item D	Item E
Ceiling (NRV)	$61	$85	$55	$107	$55
– Normal mark-up	–10	–12	–15	– 22	–15
Floor	**$51**	**$73**	**$40**	**$ 85**	**$40**

When you know the ceiling and the floor, you can determine LCM:

Item	Cost*	Replacement cost	Ceiling (NRV)	Floor	Market	Item at LCM	
A $64		$ 63	$ 61	$51	$ 61[1]	$ 61	(m)
B 82		80	85	73	80[2]	80	(m)
C 38		37	55	40	40[3]	38	(c)
D 95		109	107	85	107[4]	95	(c)
E 47		39	55	40	40[5]	+ 40	(m)
			Ending inventory applying LCM item by item			$314	

* Given.

The following notes are explanatory and were not required in the answer:

1. **Item A:** The $63 replacement cost was higher than the ceiling of $61, so the ceiling became market. The $61 market was lower than the $64 cost, so for Item A, PoCo used market.

2. **Item B:** The $80 replacement cost was below the ceiling of $85 and above the floor of $73, so the replacement cost became market. The $80 replacement cost was lower than the $82 cost, so for Item B, PoCo used market.

3. **Item C:** The $37 replacement cost was lower than the $40 floor, so the floor became market. The $38 cost was lower than the $40 market, so for Item C, PoCo used cost.

4. **Item D:** The $109 replacement cost was higher than the $107 ceiling, so the ceiling became market. The $95 cost was lower than the $107 ceiling, so for Item D, PoCo used cost.

5. **Item E:** The replacement cost of $39 was lower than the $40 floor, so the floor became market. The $40 market was lower than the $47 cost, so for Item E, PoCo used market.

Problem II.

Item	Total units	Unit at LCM	Total at LCM
Wooden chairs...... 100		$67	$ 6,700 (m)
Metal chairs 300		33	9,900 (c)
Plastic chairs....... 600		13	7,800 (c)
Beach chairs 500		11	+ 5,500 (c)
Ending inventory applying LCM item by item			**$29,900**

Problem III.

Item	Total units	Unit at cost	Item at cost	Unit at market	Item at market
AM 400		$20	$ 8,000	$22	$ 8,800
AM/FM 600		53	31,800	49	29,400
AM with alarm.......... 500		36	18,000	34	17,000
A/FM with alarm........ 900		77	+ 69,300	78	+ 70,200
Ending inventory—all items at cost			**$127,100**		
Ending inventory—all items at market					**$125,400**

Applying LCM to total inventory, DiCo's ending inventory is $125,400.

Problem IV.

Product	Number of units	Unit at cost	Item at cost	Class at cost	Unit at market	Item at market	Class at market	Class at LCM
Residential								
Sofas 10		$280	$ 2,800		$250	$ 2,500		
Armchairs 30		140	+ 4,200		160	+ 4,800		
. . . .				$ 7,000			$ 7,300	$ 7,000 (c)
Office								
Desks 40		190	7,600		170	6,800		
Bookcases 50		110	5,500		120	6,000		
Swivel chairs 30		220	+ 6,600		205	+ 6,150		
. . . .				$19,700			$18,950	$18,950 (m)
Commercial								
Display cases 70		400	28,000		410	28,700		
Chairs 80		90	+ 7,200		70	+ 5,600		
				$35,200			$34,300	+$34,300 (m)

Ending inventory applying LCM by class $60,250

Problem V.

December 4, 20X5
There is no entry because making a commitment to buy is not an accountable event.

December 31, 20X5

Estimated Loss on Purchase Commitment	3,000*	
Estimated Liability on Purchase Commitment		3,000

* 1,000 ounces to be purchased x $19 commitment price per ounce = $19,000 commitment price.
1,000 ounces to be purchased x $16 market price per ounce = $16,000 cost at market.
$19,000 commitment price – $16,000 year-end market price = $3,000 loss on market decline.

February 23, 20X6

Inventory	18,000**	
Estimated Liability on Purchase Commitment	3,000	
Recovery of Loss on Purchase		
Commitment		2,000***
Accounts Payable		19,000****

** 1,000 ounces x $18 market price per ounce = $18,000 cost basis.
*** $18,000 cost basis on February 23, 20X6 – $16,000 market value on December 31, 20X6 = $2,000 recovery of market decline from purchase commitment.
**** $19,000 is the amount due because price set in the purchase commitment was $19 per ounce x 1,000 ounces.

March 22, 20X6

Accounts Payable	19,000	
Cash		19,000

QUIZ 2 INVENTORY COSTING USING THE LOWER OF COST OR MARKET RULE

Problem I.

On December 31, 20X8, FiCo shows the following data for ending inventory:

Item	Cost*	Replacement cost	Selling price	Disposal cost	Normal mark-up
A	$320	$310	$450	$35	$80
B	450	370	500	40	100
C	225	200	325	80	60
D	300	270	380	40	50
E	460	560	600	50	100

* Given.

1. Determine market for each item.

2. Compute ending inventory applying LCM item by item.

Problem II.

On December 31, 20X6, MoCo's inventory consists of the following:

Item	Total units	Unit at cost	Unit at market
Wooden bats	200	$22	$27
Metal bats	600	17	15
Plastic bats	700	9	8
Foam bats	900	5	7

Calculate MoCo's ending inventory applying LCM item by item.

Problem III.

On December 31, 20X9, DiCo's ending inventory is as follows:

Item	Total cases	Unit at cost	Unit at market
Oregano	1,400	$32	$29
Basil	2,600	63	59
Pepper...........	1,500	46	43
Cloves	900	77	80

What is DiCo's ending inventory applying LCM to total inventory?

Problem IV.

As of December 31, 20X9, XeCo's inventory has three classes of merchandise holding seven items in total, as follows:

Class/item	Total units	Unit at cost	Unit at market
Clothing			
Jerseys	900	$ 58	$ 55
Pants.	700	73	78
Equipment			
Balls	1,500	19	16
Tennis rackets	50	210	230
Hockey sticks	200	190	180
Accessories			
First-aid kits	300	50	55
Sunglasses.	600	30	20

Calculate XeCo's ending inventory on December 31, 20X9, applying LCM by class.

Problem V.

On October 20, 20X7, VaCo signs a $77,000 purchase commitment for merchandise to be delivered in January, 20X8. On December 31, 20X7, when VaCo prepares its financial statements, the market price is $73,000. On January 10, 20X8, when the merchandise is delivered C.O.D., the market price is $70,000.

Prepare the entries that VaCo must use to record these events.

QUIZ 2   Solutions and Explanations

Problem I.

1. To compute market, you must first compute the ceiling and the floor:

	Item A	Item B	Item C	Item D	Item E
Selling price (given)	$450	$500	$325	$380	$600
– Disposal cost	– 35	– 40	– 80	– 40	– 50
Ceiling (NRV)	**$415**	**$460**	**$245**	**$340**	**$550**

	Item A	Item B	Item C	Item D	Item E
Ceiling (NRV)	$415	$460	$245	$340	$550
– Normal mark-up*	– 80	–100	– 60	– 50	–100
Floor	**$335**	**$360**	**$185**	**$290**	**$450**

* Given.

2. When you know the ceiling and floor, you can determine lower of cost or market item by item for total inventory:

Item	Cost*	Replacement cost	Ceiling (NRV)	Floor	Market	Item at LCM	
A.........	$320	$310	$415	$335	$335[1]	$ 320	(c)
B.........	450	370	460	360	370[2]	370	(m)
C.........	225	200	245	185	200[3]	200	(m)
D.........	300	270	340	290	290[4]	290	(m)
E.........	460	560	550	450	550[5]	+ 460	(c)
			Ending inventory applying LCM by item			$1,640	

* Given.

The following notes are explanatory and were not required in the answer:

1. **Item A:** The $310 replacement cost was lower than the $335 floor, so the floor became market. The $320 cost was lower than than the $335 market, so for Item A, FiCo used cost.

2. **Item B:** The $370 replacement cost was lower then the $460 ceiling and higher than the $360 floor, so the replacement cost became market. The $370 market was lower than the $450 cost, so for Item B, FiCo used market.

3. **Item C:** The $200 replacement cost was lower than the $245 ceiling and higher than the $185 floor, so the replacement cost became market. The $200 market was lower than the $225 cost, so for Item C, FiCo used market.

4. **Item D:** The $270 replacement cost was lower than the $290 floor, so the floor became market. The $270 market was lower than the $300 cost, so for Item D, FiCo used market.

5. **Item E:** The $560 replacement cost was higher than the $550 ceiling, so the ceiling became market. The $460 cost was lower than the $550 market, so for Item E, FiCo used cost.

Problem II.

Item	Total units	Unit at LCM	Item at LCM
Wooden bats 200		$22	$ 4,400 (c)
Metal bats 600		15	9,000 (m)
Plastic bats 700		8	5,600 (m)
Foam bats 900		5	+ 4,500 (c)
Ending inventory applying LCM item by item			**$23,500**

Problem III.

Item	Number of cases	Case at cost	Item at cost	Case at market	Item at market
Oregano.............. 1,400		$32	$ 44,800	$29	$ 40,600
Basil................. 2,600		63	163,800	59	153,400
Pepper 1,500		46	69,000	43	64,500
Cloves 900		77	69,300	80	72,000
Ending inventory—all items at cost			**$346,900**		
Ending inventory—all items at market					**$330,500**

DiCo's ending inventory applying LCM to all items in inventory is $330,500.

Problem IV.

Class/item	Total units	Unit at cost	Total at cost	Unit at cost	Total at market	LCM by class
Clothing						
Jerseys	900	$ 58	$ 52,200	$ 55	$ 49,500	
Pants	700	73	+ 51,100	78	+ 54,600	
Total for class.			$103,300		$104,100	$103,300 (c)
Equipment						
Balls.	1,500	19	$ 28,500	16	$ 24,000	
Tennis rackets	50	210	10,500	230	11,500	
Hockey sticks	200	190	+ 38,000	180	+ 36,000	
Total for class.			$ 77,000		$ 71,500	$ 71,500 (m)
Accessories						
First-aid kits	300	50	15,000	55	$ 16,500	
Sunglasses	600	30	18,000	20	12,000	
Total for class.			$ 33,000		$ 28,500	$ 28,500 (m)
			Ending inventory applying LCM by class			$203,300

Problem V.

October 20, 20X7

There is no entry because a commitment to buy is not an accountable event.

December 31, 20X7

Estimated Loss on Purchase Commitment	4,000*	
Estimated Liability on Purchase Commitment		4,000

* $77,000 commitment price – $73,000 year-end market price = $4,000 loss on market decline.

January 10, 20X8

Inventory	70,000	
Loss on Purchase Commitment	3,000*	
Estimated Liability on Purchase Commitment	4,000	
Cash		77,000

* $73,000 year-end market price – $70,000 delivery date market price = $3,000 loss on market decline.

Final Examination (Optional)
MASTERING INVENTORY

Instructions: Detach the Final Examination Answer Sheet on page 215 before beginning your final examination. Select the correct letter for the answer to each multiple choice question below, and then mark it on the Answer Sheet. Allow approximately $2\frac{1}{2}$ hours.

1. BaCo opens its business in 20X2 and purchases merchandise on account for $88,000. In 20X2, BaCo pays $67,000 cash on the $88,000 due, sales are $145,000, and ending inventory is $24,000. BaCo's gross profit for 20X2 is . . .

   a. $102,000   b. $81,000   c. $78,000   d. $57,000

2. GeCo begins 20X4 with merchandise costing $69,000. 20X4 sales are $233,000, purchases are $198,000, and ending inventory is $81,000. GeCo's 20X4 cost of goods sold is . . .

   a. $245,000   b. $221,000   c. $210,000   d. $186,000

3. On December 3, HuCo purchases merchandise for $47,000 on account, F.O.B. destination. Freight charges are $800. On December 26, HuCo pays the vendor $14,000. On HuCo's December 31 balance sheet the accounts payable balance will be . . .

   a. $33,800   b. $47,000   c. $47,800   d. $33,000

4. RiCo uses the perpetual method for inventory and records purchases at gross. In 20X4, it has total merchandise purchases of $324,000. It returns $19,000 of the merchandise for full credit and receives $7,000 in allowances from its vendors for defective merchandise and takes cash discounts of $1,000. The net cost of RiCo's 20X4 merchandise purchases is . . .

   a. $297,000   b. $305,000   c. $324,000   d. $298,000

5. LoCo, which uses the periodic method, purchases merchandise on account for $56,000, F.O.B. shipping point. Freight charges are $900 C.O.D. LoCo should record these purchases as . . .

a. Purchases   56,000
    Accounts Payable   55,100
    Cash   900

b. Purchases   56,900
    Accounts Payable   56,000
    Cash   900

c. Purchases   56,000
  Freight-In   900
    Accounts Payable   56,000
    Cash   900

d. Purchases   55,100
  Freight-In   900
    Accounts Payable   55,100
    Cash   900

6. PiCo uses the perpetual method. On February 17, PiCo sells $30,000 in merchandise on account that cost $10,000. On February 23, 10% of these goods are returned. Prepare the entry that PiCo makes on February 23 to record the sales return.

a. Sales Returns   3,000
    Accounts Receivable   3,000

b. Sales Returns   1,000
    Gross Profit   2,000
    Accounts Receivable   3,000

c. Sales Returns   3,000
    Accounts Receivable   3,000

  Inventory   1,000
    Cost of Goods Sold   1,000

d. Sales Returns   3,000
    Accounts Receivable   3,000

  Inventory   1,000
    Purchase Returns   1,000

7. VeCo, which uses the perpetual method, records merchandise purchases at gross. On October 3, VeCo buys $42,000 of merchandise on account. Terms are 2/10, n/40. On October 9, VeCo returns goods that cost $10,000. On October 11, VeCo pays $31,360. What entry does VeCo record on October 11?

a. Accounts Payable   31,360
    Cash   31,360

b. Accounts Payable   32,000
    Cash   31,360
    Purchase Discounts   640

c. Accounts Payable   32,000
    Cash   31,360
    Inventory   640

d. Accounts Payable   31,360
    Purchase Discounts   640
    Cash   31,360
    Inventory   640

8. MoCo begins operations in April, uses the perpetual method, and records merchandise purchases at net. MoCo makes two purchases on account. Terms are 1/15, n/45. On April 4, MoCo purchases merchandise for $3,000, which it pays for on April 16. On April 11, it makes a $9,000 purchase that it pays for on April 29, but there are no sales in April. On April 30, the balance in MoCo's inventory ledger account is . . .

    a. $12,000   b. $11,970   c. $11,880   d. $11,910

9. XaCo begins business in June and uses the periodic method. Its June merchandise purchases are $195,000 on account, F.O.B. shipping point. Merchandise that cost $3,000 is returned for credit. Goods that XaCo sells for $11,000 and that cost $7,000 are returned to XaCo for cash refunds. On July 6, XaCo pays a $6,000 freight bill for its June purchases. The net cost of XaCo's June purchases is . . .

    a. $205,000   b. $198,000   c. $192,000   d. $209,000

10. YiCo buys 800 cases of tennis balls listed at $130 per case and for which YiCo is given a 15% volume discount. YiCo sells 70% of the cases for cash. The cost of the *unsold* merchandise is . . .

    a. $15,600   b. $31,200   c. $26,520   d. $77,350

11. JaCo uses the periodic method and records merchandise purchases at net. Its 20X4 ending inventory is $69,000. During 20X5, JaCo purchases merchandise for $878,000, with freight-in of $11,000. Purchase returns are $17,000, purchase discounts lost are $4,000, and the cost of merchandise on hand at year end is $91,000. At year end, JaCo records the following entry:

a.	Ending Inventory	91,000	
	Purchase Returns	17,000	
	Cost of Goods Sold	850,000	
	Purchases		878,000
	Freight-In		11,000
	Beginning Inventory		69,000
b.	Ending Inventory	91,000	
	Purchase Returns	17,000	
	Cost of Goods Sold	846,000	
	Purchase Discounts Lost	4,000	
	Purchases		878,000
	Freight-In		11,000
	Beginning Inventory		69,000
c.	Ending Inventory	91,000	
	Purchase Returns	17,000	
	Cost of Goods Sold	854,000	
	Purchases		878,000
	Freight-In		11,000
	Beginning Inventory		69,000
	Purchase Discounts Lost		4,000
d.	Beginning Inventory	69,000	
	Purchase Returns	17,000	
	Cost of Goods Sold	894,000	
	Purchases		878,000
	Freight-In		11,000
	Ending Inventory		91,000

12. NuCo uses the periodic method and has the following account balances: Purchase Returns, $17,000; Beginning Inventory, $4,000; Purchases, $193,000; Freight-In, $11,000; and Accounts Payable, $23,000. What are NuCo's net purchases?

    a. $187,000   b. $191,000   c. $183,000   d. $210,000

13. WeCo has the following account balances: Purchase Returns, $19,000; Purchases, $812,000; Purchase Discounts, $8,000; Beginning Inventory, $21,000; Freight-In, $30,000; and Ending Inventory, $37,000. WeCo's cost of goods sold is . . .

    a. $769,000   b. $783,000   c. $815,000   d. $799,000

14. JiCo uses the periodic method. Its beginning inventory is $43,000, purchases are $321,000, F.O.B. destination, purchase returns are $17,000, and freight is $9,000. The balance in JiCo's ledger Purchases account is . . .

    a. $330,000   b. $317,000   c. $321,000   d. $304,000

15. VaCo, which uses the periodic method, is preparing its year-end journal entry to record cost of goods sold. It debits all of the following accounts *except* . . .

    a. Cost of Goods Sold
    b. Beginning Inventory
    c. Purchase Discounts
    d. None of the above

16. SeCo begins operations in 20X6 and uses the periodic method and weighted-average costing. SeCo has the following merchandise purchases during 20X6: 700 units in March @ $4; 1,100 units in July @ $6; and 2,200 units in October @ $7. A physical count of ending inventory finds 1,000 units. Calculate the cost of goods sold.

    a. $6,200   b. $7,000   c. $18,600   d. $24,000

17. FoCo uses the periodic method and weighted-average costing. The cost of the 2,500 units in FoCo's 20X3 ending inventory is $32,500. FoCo has the following merchandise purchases during 20X4: 1,700 units in May @ $14; 3,500 units in June @ $19; and 2,300 in October @ $21. Calculate the cost of the 1,200 units in ending inventory.

    a. $20,532   b. $16,632   c. $22,176   d. $25,200

18. LiCo uses the periodic method and weighted-average costing. On December 31, 20X7, LiCo's inventory consists of 1,800 units costing $5 each. In January, 20X8, LiCo purchases 4,000 units @ $9, of which it returns 700 units in March. It purchases 4,400 units in October @ $7, of which it returns 500 units in December. The weighted-average cost per unit of goods available for sale during 20X8 is . . .

    a. $7.92   b. $7.33   c. $6.47   d. $6.79

19. TuCo begins operations in 20X1 and uses the perpetual method and moving average costing. On January 4, TuCo buys 1,200 units of merchandise @ $3. On January 8, it sells 300 units. On January 11, it buys 1,100 units @ $4, and on January 30, it sells 600 units. On January 30, what does TuCo record as the cost of goods sold?

    a. $2,430   b. $2,130   c. $2,400   d. $1,800

20. XoCo, which begins business in May and uses the perpetual method and moving average costing, shows the following data:

	Purchases	Sales
May 4	1,000 @ $ 7	
May 11		400 @ $11
May 14	1,400 @ $ 8	
May 19	2,000 @ $10	
May 21		1,500 @ $15

    The balance in XoCo's inventory account on May 31 is . . .

    a. $22,125   b. $20,833   c. $21,705   d. $23,875

21. MaCo begins operations in 20X1 and uses the periodic method and FIFO costing. In March, 20X1, MaCo buys 700 units @ $4; in July, it buys 2,700 units @ $6, and in November, it buys 1,600 units @ $8. The cost of the 1,900 units in MaCo's December 31 ending inventory is . . .

    a. $10,000   b. $15,200   c. $14,600   d. $7,600

22. JoCo uses the periodic method and FIFO costing. JoCo's December 31, 20X2 inventory consists of 400 units bought in November, 20X2 @ $11. During 20X3, JoCo made the following purchases: 1,800 units @ $14 in January; 2,200 units @ $17 in July; and 2,300 units @ $13 in October. The December 31, 20X3 inventory consists of 1,300 units. JoCo's 20X3 cost of goods sold is . . .

    a. $80,000   b. $79,900   c. $80,800   d. $78,700

23. NiCo begins operations in 20X4, makes all sales on account, uses the perpetual method and FIFO costing, and shows the following data:

	Purchases	**Sales**
February 4	700 @ $ 7	
May 11		400 @ $15
July 14	1,100 @ $ 8	
September 19	3,000 @ $10	
December 21		1,500 @ $18

On December 21, what entries does NiCo record?

a. Accounts Receivable   27,000
      Sales   27,000

    Cost of Goods Sold   15,000
      Inventory   15,000

b. Accounts Receivable   27,000
      Sales   27,000

    Cost of Goods Sold   9,200
      Inventory   9,200

c. Accounts Receivable   27,000
      Sales   27,000

    Cost of Goods Sold   11,900
      Inventory   11,900

d. Accounts Receivable   27,000
      Sales   27,000

    Cost of Goods Sold   12,000
      Inventory   12,000

24. TeCo uses the perpetual method and FIFO costing. TeCo's December 31, 20X5 inventory consists of 800 units @ $7. In 20X6, TeCo's merchandise purchases and sales are as follows:

	Purchases	**Sales**
February 24	1,700 @ $ 9	
June 11		2,000 @ $25
August 17	2,100 @ $11	
September 1		1,600 @ $28
October 19	3,000 @ $14	
November 29		2,700 @ $30

TeCo's December 31, 20X6 ending inventory is . . .

    a. $18,200   b. $12,600   c. $11,700   d. $10,100

25. PaCo begins business in 20X3, uses the periodic method and LIFO costing and makes the following merchandise purchases:

January 14	1,300 @ $50
March 11	2,800 @ $55
August 23	1,700 @ $58
November 1	1,200 @ $60

If PaCo's December 31, 20X3 inventory contains 1,500 units, its ending inventory is . . .

    a. $89,400   b. $76,000   c. $90,000   d. $75,000

26. MiCo opens for business in 20X3 and uses the periodic method and LIFO costing. On December 31, 20X3, there are 900 units of merchandise in MiCo's inventory @ $11. MiCo's 20X4 merchandise purchases are as follows:

February 4	1,200 @ $14
March 10	2,000 @ $15
July 7	3,300 @ $18
October 21	4,200 @ $20

If MiCo's December 31, 20X4 physical count shows 1,500 units in ending inventory, then ending inventory on MiCo's balance sheet will be . . .

a. $21,300   b. $30,000   c. $18,300   d. $21,900

27. CuCo, which begins business in 20X8, uses the periodic method and LIFO costing. CuCo's 20X8 merchandise purchases are as follows:

January 3	2,200 @ $5
April 16	1,800 @ $8
September 25	3,000 @ $6
December 4	1,100 @ $9

If CuCo's December 31, 20X8 ending inventory is 300 units, its 20X8 cost of goods sold is . . .

a. $51,800   b. $50,600   c. $49,900   d. $52,100

28. KoCo begins operations in 20X1 and uses the periodic method. In March, 20X1, KoCo buys 700 units @ $4; in July, it buys 2,700 units @ $6; and in November, it buys 1,600 units @ $8. Using LIFO, what is the cost of the 1,900 units in ending inventory?

a. $10,000   b. $15,200   c. $14,600   d. $7,600

29. SiCo begins operations in 20X2 and uses the periodic method. SiCo's December 31, 20X2 ending inventory consists of 400 units bought in January, 20X2 @ $11. Its December 31, 20X3 ending inventory consists of 1,300 units. During January, 20X3, SiCo buys 1,800 units @ $14; in July, it buys 2,200 units @ $17; and in October, it buys 2,300 units @ $13. If SiCo uses LIFO, its 20X3 costs of goods sold is . . .

a. $80,000   b. $79,900   c. $80,800   d. $78,700

Use the following information for problems #30–33.

LuCo begins operations in 20X4 and uses the periodic method and LIFO costing. Its merchandise purchases are as follows:

	20X4	**20X5**	**20X6**
March	300 @ $4	600 @ $ 8	900 @ $11
July	500 @ $5	900 @ $12	600 @ $14
September	200 @ $7	100 @ $ 9	700 @ $13
November	400 @ $6	700 @ $10	100 @ $16

30. If LuCo sells 900 units in 20X4, its December 31, 20X4 ending inventory of 500 units is . . .

a. $2,000   b. $3,000   c. $2,200   d. $3,100

31. If, instead, LuCo's has 200 units in its December 31, 20X4 ending inventory and 500 units in its December 31, 20X5 ending inventory, then its December 31, 20X5 inventory is . . .

a. $3,200   b. $4,000   c. $5,000   d. $2,200

32. Assume, instead, that LuCo's December 31, 20X4 ending inventory is 300 units; its December 31, 20X5 ending inventory is 200 units (which is lower than it 20X5 beginning inventory); and its December 31, 20X6 ending inventory is 700 units. What is LuCo's December 31, 20X6 inventory?

a. $7,700   b. $4,400   c. $5,600   d. $6,300

33. Assume, instead, that LuCo's December 31, 20X4 ending inventory is 300 units; its December 31, 20X5 ending inventory is 800 units; and its December 31, 20X6 ending inventory is 600 units (which is lower than its 20X6 beginning inventory). What is LuCo's December 31, 20X6 ending inventory?

    a. $6,600   b. $4,800   c. $4,400   d. $3,600

34. When WeCo begins operations in 20X4, it chooses the periodic method and LIFO costing. Within a given year's LIFO layer, it uses weighted average costing. During 20X4, WeCo makes the following merchandise purchases:

May 30	400 @ $4
June 24	800 @ $5
October 11	900 @ $7
December 4	1,400 @ $6

    If the December 31, 20X4 ending inventory is 1,000 units, and the December 31, 20X5 ending inventory is 300 units, what is the 20X5 ending inventory?

    a. $1,200   b. $1,380   c. $1,740   d. $1,800

Use the following information for problems #35–40.

HuCo begins operations in 20X4, uses the periodic method and makes the following merchandise purchases:

20X4	Total units	Unit cost	Total cost
April	900	$ 6	$5,400
September	1,300	7	9,100
20X5			
March	1,100	$ 8	$8,800
November	500	10	5,000

35. If HuCo uses FIFO costing and its December 31, 20X5 ending inventory is 800 units, then ending inventory on its balance sheet will be . . .

    a. $8,800   b. $5,600   c. $9,400   d. $7,400

36. If HuCo uses LIFO costing and sold 2,000 units in 20X4, what is its cost of goods sold?

    a. $14,000   b. $13,300   c. $13,100   d. $13,000

37. If HuCo uses LIFO costing and sold 1,700 units each year, what is its 20X5 cost of goods sold?

    a. $14,300   b. $12,700   c. $14,400   d. $12,800

38. Assume that HuCo uses LIFO costing. It sold 1,500 units in 20X4 and has 1,000 units in its December 31, 20X5 ending inventory. What is ending inventory on its December 31, 20X5 balance sheet?

    a. $6,600   b. $8,000   c. $6,200   d. $7,000

39. If HuCo uses FIFO costing and sold 1,800 units each year, what is its 20X5 cost of goods sold?

    a. $14,200   b. $10,700   c. $14,600   d. $10,300

40. HuCo, which uses weighted average costing, has 700 units in 20X4 ending inventory. If HuCo sells 1,600 units in 20X5, what is its 20X5 cost of goods sold (round unit costs in the computation to the nearest penny)?

    a. $13,800   b. $11,040   c. $11,760   d. $12,816

Use the following information for problems #41–43.

TiCo has 1,000 units of merchandise on hand at year end. Each unit cost $32, has a replacement cost of $29, has an estimated selling price of $42, has a disposal cost of $4, and has an estimated normal mark-up of $7.

41. If TiCo applies the lower of cost or market (LCM) rule, what is the ceiling or upper limit?

    a. $29   b. $25   c. $28   d. $38

42. Applying LCM, what floor or lower limit must TiCo use?

a. $31   b. $35   c. $32   d. $29

43. Assume that the ceiling for each unit is $33 and the floor is $27. What per unit amount will TiCo use for ending inventory on its balance sheet?

a. $32   b. $29   c. $33   d. $27

Use the following information for problems #44–46.

JaCo has the following inventory at year end:

	Cases on hand	Cost per case	Market per case
Plastic			
Cars and trucks	12	$80	$75
Action figures	18	22	28
Rubber			
Pool toys	20	$56	$62
Sports novelties	80	32	29
Zoo animals	110	17	15
Cardboard			
Board games	30	$34	$24
Jigsaw puzzles	50	21	23

44. What is JaCo's ending inventory applying LCM by item?

a. $8,156   b. $8,484   c. $8,358   d. $8,436

45. What is JaCo's ending inventory applying LCM by group?

a. $8,156   b. $8,484   c. $8,358   d. $8,436

46. What is JaCo's ending inventory applying LCM to total inventory?

    a. $8,156   b. $8,484   c. $8,358   d. $8,436

Use the following information for problems #47–48.

Applying LCM, NeCo determines that as of December 31, 20X3, merchandise that originally cost $46,300 is now $43,500 at market.

47. NeCo determines that the loss is not material enough to warrant disclosure as a line item on its income statement. Therefore it should . . .

    a. make no entry but disclose the loss in a note on the financial statements.
    b. make no entry and make no disclosure.
    c. make an entry to reduce retained earnings.
    d. make an entry to increase cost of goods sold.

48. Early in 20X4, the market value of NeCo's inventory unexpectedly increases to $47,500. If the original credit to write-down inventory was to the Inventory account, NeCo should . . .

    a. recognize a $4,000 gain.
    b. recognize a $2,800 gain.
    c. make no entry but disclose the loss in a note accompanying the financial statements.
    d. make no entry and make no disclosure.

Use the following information for problems #49–50.

On December 4, 20X8, DoCo enters into a contractual agreement to take delivery on January 25, 20X9 of 10,000 pounds of nuts at a cost of $2.20 per pound. On December 31, 20X8, DoCo finds that the market price of the nuts has declined to $1.90 per pound, and management decides that the decline is permanent.

49. DoCo should show these developments on its 20X8 financial statements as . . .

    a. a $22,000 liability
    b. a $19,000 liability
    c. a $3,000 liability
    d. no liability

50. When DoCo takes delivery on January 25, 20X9, the market price of nuts is $1.75 per pound. As a result, DoCo should . . .

    a. debit Inventory $17,500
    b. debit Inventory $22,000
    c. debit Loss $4,500
    d. debit Retained Earnings $3,000

Final Examination Answer Sheet
MASTERING INVENTORY

Instructions: Detach this sheet before starting the Final Exam. For each question, check the box beneath the letter of the correct answer. Use a #2 pencil to make a dark impression. When completed, return to: AIPB Continuing Education, Suite 500, 6001 Montrose Road, Rockville, MD 20852. If you attain a grade of at least 70, you will receive the Institute's *Certificate of Completion*. Answer Sheets are not returned.

Certified Bookkeeper applicants: If you attain a grade of at least 70, and become certified within 3 years of passing this exam, you will receive retroactively ten (10) Continuing Professional Education Credits (CPECs) toward your *Certified Bookkeeper* CPEC requirements.

1. a b c d ☐☐☐☐	14. a b c d ☐☐☐☐	27. a b c d ☐☐☐☐	39. a b c d ☐☐☐☐
2. a b c d ☐☐☐☐	15. a b c d ☐☐☐☐	28. a b c d ☐☐☐☐	40. a b c d ☐☐☐☐
3. a b c d ☐☐☐☐	16. a b c d ☐☐☐☐	29. a b c d ☐☐☐☐	41. a b c d ☐☐☐☐
4. a b c d ☐☐☐☐	17. a b c d ☐☐☐☐	30. a b c d ☐☐☐☐	42. a b c d ☐☐☐☐
5. a b c d ☐☐☐☐	18. a b c d ☐☐☐☐	31. a b c d ☐☐☐☐	43. a b c d ☐☐☐☐
6. a b c d ☐☐☐☐	19. a b c d ☐☐☐☐	32. a b c d ☐☐☐☐	44. a b c d ☐☐☐☐
7. a b c d ☐☐☐☐	20. a b c d ☐☐☐☐	33. a b c d ☐☐☐☐	45. a b c d ☐☐☐☐
8. a b c d ☐☐☐☐	21. a b c d ☐☐☐☐	34. a b c d ☐☐☐☐	46. a b c d ☐☐☐☐
9. a b c d ☐☐☐☐	22. a b c d ☐☐☐☐	35. a b c d ☐☐☐☐	47. a b c d ☐☐☐☐
10. a b c d ☐☐☐☐	23. a b c d ☐☐☐☐	36. a b c d ☐☐☐☐	48. a b c d ☐☐☐☐
11. a b c d ☐☐☐☐	24. a b c d ☐☐☐☐	37. a b c d ☐☐☐☐	49. a b c d ☐☐☐☐
12. a b c d ☐☐☐☐	25. a b c d ☐☐☐☐	38. a b c d ☐☐☐☐	50. a b c d ☐☐☐☐
13. a b c d ☐☐☐☐	26. a b c d ☐☐☐☐		

Name (Please print clearly.)   Title

Company   Street Address

City   State   Zip

For *Certified Bookkeeper* applicants only: #_____

Membership or Certification (nonmember) ID Number

Course Evaluation for
MASTERING INVENTORY

Please complete and return (even if you do not take the Final Examination) to: AIPB Continuing Education, Suite 500, 6001 Montrose Road, Rockville, MD 20852. **PLEASE PRINT CLEARLY.**

Circle one

1. Did you find the instructions clear?   Yes   No

Comments:

_____

_____

2. Did you find the course practical?   Yes   No

Comments

_____

_____

3. Is this course what you expected?   Yes   No

Comments

_____

_____

4. Would you recommend this course to other accounting professionals?   Yes   No

Comments:

_____

_____

5. What did you like most about *Mastering Inventory*? _____

_____

6. What would have made the course even more helpful? _____

_____

7. May we use your comments and name in advertising for the course?   Yes   No

8. Would you be interested in other courses?   Yes   No

Please indicate what subject areas would be of greatest interest to you: _____

1. _____   3. _____

2. _____   4. _____

_____
Name (optional)   Title

_____
Company   Street Address

_____
City   State   Zip   Phone Number

NOTES